MBA IS FUN DA

Kumara Swamy. N

MBA IS FUN DA
Copyright © 2014 Kumara Swamy. N
All rights reserved

No part of this publication may be reproduced, stored in a retrieval system, or transmitted, in any form or by means electronic, mechanical, photocopying, or otherwise, without prior written permission of the publisher.

Requests for permission should be addressed to
Kumara Swamy. N (kumarthestar@gmail.com).

Contents

Contents		3
1	Customer Service	19
2	Fast Moving Consumer Goods (FMCG)	21
3	Time Management	25
4	Life Style Management	27
5	Stress Management	29
6	How to be a Good Speaker & Improve Your Communication Skills.	31
7	Marketing Management - Tap the Market Before Someone Does	33
8	Fast Moving Consumer Durables Sector (FMCD)	37
9	Moral Science: Mother Earth	39

10 Indian Society - Indian Ethos and Values in Modern Management	41
11 Business Communication	43
12 Human Resource Management	45
13 Knowledge Management	47
14 World of Beauty Salons	49
15 A for Aim and A for Archery	51
16 Summer Project	53
17 Organization Study	55
18 Out of home consumption - The Food Business	57
19 Shelter Business - The Real Estate	59
20 Psychology	61
21 Automobile Industry	63
22 Insurance Industry	67
23 Banking Industry	69
24 Jewellery Business	71
25 ITES Industry	73
26 Hospital Management	75
27 Hotel Management	77

28	Customer Relationship Management	79
29	Industrial Relations	81
30	Service Management	85
31	Retail Management	87
32	Self Defense	91
33	Finance	93
34	Dance and Music	95
35	Human Resource Consulting Business	97
36	Online Marketing	99
37	International Business	101
38	Entrepreneurship	103
39	Small and Medium Enterprises	105
40	Advertising Management	107
41	Moral Science - Love trees	109
42	Telecom & Mobiles	111
43	Principles of Management	113
44	Consumer Behavior	115
45	Body Language	117
46	Organization Behavior	119

47	Strategic Management	121
48	Human Relations Skills	123
49	Employee Counseling	125
50	Supply Chain & Distribution Management	127
51	B2B	129
52	International Marketing	131
53	Yoga	133
54	Brand Management	135
55	Marketing Research	137
56	International Human Resource Management	139
57	Labor Laws	141
58	Corporate Gifting	143
59	Compensation Management	145
60	Performance Management	147
61	Modern Manager	149
62	Sales Management	151
63	Event Management	153
64	Rural Marketing	155
65	Economics	157

66 Being Artistic -
   Sketch-Draw-Paint-Craft   159

67 Moral Science - Social Service   161

68 Playing with Numbers & Data - Business Maths & Statistics   163

69 Business Law   165

70 MIS   167

71 Production Management   169

72 Happy Employees Happy Company   171

73 Leadership   173

74 Mutual Funds   175

75 Materials Management   177

76 Show Business   179

77 Fitness Industry - Six Packs Management   181

78 Love Cricket - Cricket makes us Not Out for Life   183

79 Luxury Brand Management   185

80 Business Ethics   189

81 Business Environment   191

82 Wealth Management   193

83 Talent Management   195

84 Training & Development	197
85 Corporate Image Management	199
86 Management Consulting	201
87 Negotiation	203
88 Quality Management Systems	205
89 Business Ideas	207
90 Operations Research	209
91 Work Experience	211
92 Business Icons	213
93 Raw Materials	215
94 Around the World - Tourism Industry	217
95 Bulls & Bears - Understanding Stock Markets	219
96 Franchisee Business	221
97 Merger & Acquisition	223
98 Go Getter	225
99 Racing	227
100 Business Schools	229

*This book, MBA IS FUN Da,
is dedicated to all management lovers
and to my parents who brought me down
to this beautiful planet - Planet India.*

Preface

Everyone likes to know about management. So this book covers all the management subjects and various industries in brief. Some special topics on moral Science & self improvement topics are also included in this book - MBA is FUN Da.

MBA is FUN Da, makes you learn & implement things faster. Most of my writing was from my own experiences after working with different industries. All these years, I have spent my time understanding different industries so it was easy to bring all in one place. This book is my sincere knowledge transfer to management buddies. This book makes you a real life super corporate rock star. This book includes Indian examples; this book is a complete informative entertainer. This book is a fun way to teach yourself management. But I recommend further reading, because management subjects are fun and exciting, and learning never ends. So learn more from your teachers and corporate & the book also helps one to choose your favorite sector & specialization to work or to do business.

At the beginning of every chapter you can find 'Guru'. Reason is, I cannot forget my Gurus & the God, who taught me management. After reading this book 'MBA is FUN Da', you will be happy in life, and you will also be confident to face real life business situations easily.

This book will help students who like to join MBA programs, students of under-graduate & post-graduate - management studies, management teachers, and management lovers and businessmen.

About The Author

The writer, Kumara Swamy. N, holds an MBA from Regional Institute of Co-operative Management, Bangalore. He has spent quality time working with different industries & academic institutions. He has done his summer internship with Hindustan Unilever Limited (HUL) & Coffee Day - Vending Division. He has worked for Titan Industries Limited, assignments with Tata Chemicals (Tata Salt), MTR Foods Limited, and many assignments with HUL, Myntra.com, Arvind Life Style Brands Limited, MSRCASC & other industries & B-schools. He likes to do practical knowledge transfer to everyone who approaches him.

Acknowledgement

I thank my parents, gurus, friends, relatives, society, schools, colleges, nature, companies, www, leaders, warriors, business men, birds, animals, trees, and India. I thank everyone because all have helped me to grow and all have done some knowledge transfer all these years. So I am grateful to everyone.

1 Customer Service

Customer service means to give, what a customer demands for a specific product or a service from us at the right second. Most important is to satisfy customer's requirements. Never send a customer empty-handed, you gift them something whatever possible from your side. There should be a smile on his or her face, if this happens you will get to know that he or she is satisfied.

Representative of any company handling any product or service or brands should have Gyaan about the industry which he is operating i.e., products, services. Brand gyaan is a requirement and it is a must. This makes one very strong to handle any type of customer easily.

All customers are not the same so customize your presentation as per the customer's or client's needs, so that you make a long lasting impression, and this customer, will refer a few more people, and will be loyal to you forever.

Let me tell you, customer is cash. One thing that we should remember is that our daily bread and butter comes from our customers. So give top class service to your customers, treat every customer with great respect and satisfy their needs every second = Cash for our business. Every action of ours will be converted into cash, which leads to more sales = more satisfied customers = more loyal customers = more incoming cash.

There is no bad customer or a window shopper. Every customer likes one good product or a service or something unique in our business. So it is up to us to take special care of all customers, because if a customer does not like you and your product and service, the result = wrong publicity of your business. Every customer acts like a sales manager for you by using your product and service and by referring them to his friends, so guys we have to treat all customers as equals.

Plan your day, plan your week, plan your month, plan your financial year. See what you do, how to do your business. Check where changes have to be made and customize your plans accordingly.

HAPPY CUSTOMER = HAPPY BUSINESS.

Practical Living Business Example: Everyone knows about the most famous South Indian Tiffin Room that's Mavalli Tiffin Room, popularly known as MTR, situated near lalbagh botanical garden, Namma Bengaluru. They serve quality rava, idli,vadas, mouth watering masala dosa, kesari bhath, pure filter coffee and meals. The quality is so good and the food so tasty that at MTR, customers wait for hours to a have a bite of the masala dosa. This is South India's Best Tiffin Room, all customers walk-in happily and walk out happily from many years and this tradition is going on and on.

2 Fast Moving Consumer Goods (FMCG)

Our daily needs like toothbrush, toothpaste, shaving cream, soaps, shampoos, detergents, masala powders like rasam mix, sambar mix, ready to eat snacks, chocolates, biscuits, soft drinks, tea& coffee powder, noodles, soup Mix, atta powder & much more - all these are FMCG products.

Today we see in super markets and hyper markets a huge collection of brands in their shelves, all in one roof, more options to consumers to buy these goods. Today's kids are even able to recall brand names with products, for example - Brittania biscuits, Kwality Walls ice creams, colgate - tooth paste, Parle G biscuits, Ponds - face powder, Dove - soap, Amul - cheese and butter, Bru - coffee, Cadbury - dairy milk chocolates, Complan, Boost & much more.

Look, the list is endless. We have more and more consumer goods adding every day. All brands gives us quality products, best prices and wide range of products and improve our quality of life.

Today even in our rural India, we find all brands of FMCG sector are available. REACH - to rural masses, supply chain systems of all companies are top class.

All FMCG companies operate from their factories. After the finished goods are ready, then the huge stocks are moved to their stock areas, then to carrying& forwarding agents (C& FA),then it reaches their redistribution stockiest point, then it reaches wholesalers, then to super markets, hypermarkets& retailers and finally to the end consumer.

Industry is huge, as we have a very large population in India. All companies are growing bigger and better every day, new innovation, new products each day.

Even today, the God of FMCG Sector is HUL (Hindustan Unilever Limited), HUL gives top class products to their end consumers.

Displays play a very important role in sale of FMCG products in India. Good bright appealing packaging, good POP materials (Point of Purchase), posters, danglers, in shop activity,& display windows, all these to catch the attention of the consumers. If a company does good presentation without comprising on quality, the result is more turnover. Consumers keep buying goods every day. It is a good sign for any FMCG company.

Pricing is very important in FMCG, because you cannot over price or under price a particular product. It should be reachable in the hands of every end user, so we have small packs& sachets. FMCG products are a beautiful innovation from mankind. Today all FMCG products come with packaging. So every day we are collecting large packing materials at our homes. So please buy larger packs i.e. bulk packs so that we take care of this beautiful planet where we live.

Every city has over 20,000 plus small provision stores, super market chains, hyper markets like Metro cash and carry. So business of FMCG sector is huge. In order to live longer for any brand, first thing first, connect with the consumers like Thums up, Coca cola, Tata Tea, Bru, Mysore Sandal Soaps.

Today when I visit these stores, I am very happy. Salesman is very knowledgeable and some are even taking orders on their tabs for faster deliveries. That is the beauty of an FMCG sector. They make their products available faster to the end consumer.

Employment in FMCG Sector is big. They employ people for sales, production, finance, marketing, information technology, security.

If you want to make a career in FMCG sector in sales and marketing after MBA, you can start as management trainee and you can climb the ladder till a CEO, Country Head or even be the Managing Director, or you could even start your own FMCG company. And for people who like to join FMCG sector after their graduation, they can start as entry level territory sales-in-charge or you could even work with the distributors of any FMCG brand.

I personally feel, a guy who is associated with an FMCG Industry, will create big noise in the market.

3   Time Management

TIME + Action + Interest + Energy + Effort = More cash or everyone will be more use full to society.

Every second in our life is so valuable, that all our time if utilized in the right way, can be converted into cash or gyaan, or time can be spent for doing more useful things for others.

Management of time is very important; it can be a student, working professional, businessman, or even a professor at a university or college. Time plays very important role in our life. We can't go back and make changes. If we go back and check, we would have utilized only 30% of our time, rest 70% of our time will be a waste, which could have been utilized for doing quality work for our nation - Our India.

Time management is all about making the best use of our given time, that is 24 hours, setting goals and priorities and ensuring that it will be achieved at any cost.

Society respects you, if you are a good time manager. Time machine should not be on your wrist or in your homes or at your offices. Importance of time is very serious, so wake up kids not too late, before you realize & cry for your past time. We can definitely start a new life every day, it is upto us to take special care of our time.

Time management should be programmed in such a way that it should be incorporated in our blood, no matter which blood group you belong to. So guys prepare a time action sheet everyday.

Big and most successful companies and individuals across the world have goals, objectives, and targets in mind. Hence they plan accordingly and see to it that it will be achieved at any cost.

The biggest challenge in time management is to control our minds and actions. In our journey of life, we may get many obstacles and most of the time we may not achieve what we wanted to. In India and rest of the world we blame it on fate, luck factor and most of our things are controlled by God. God gives us right paths, but our actions are not controlled. He has given enough gyaan to humans to make things work. We humans are like powerful super computers. It is how we program it - if we program it in a negative way, we waste time& not achieve anything, but if we program it in the right way or in a positive way, we may do the impossible. So guys wake up.

Practical Example of Time Management:
20: 20 - IPL Cricket matches.

Today every single day is so crucial and important& so competitive, that it is like IPL Cricket Fever, 8 hours time and lots to achieve. Do we achieve things every day? Answer is always we do not achieve. If we have to achieve our goals and objectives, program it& play your day for yourself and for others on this planet, play every day as a 20-20 match. Be responsible for your actions, every second moves so fast that it will never come back to us. In order to achieve, we need interest, dedication, preparation, contacts, knowledge, experience, guru's support. If we play every day with full force and power, we will achieve the impossible.

Best living legends who are best time managers& leaders, Shri Ratan Tata, Shri Kumar Mangalam Birla, Shri Mukesh Ambani& Shri Anil Ambani, Shri Sachin Tendulkar & also our super stars - 3 Khans of Bollywood who have given us best quality non-stop entertainment for years. This is time management.

4 Life Style Management

Life style is not to show off, its true meaning is to improve our self and improve our living conditions and make others' life comfortable& to be useful to others on this planet.

Any changes will affect our life style, hence management of our own life is in our own hands.

Positive ideas& plans within our self = Good life style = Real life hero & a role model.

Shri Ratan Tata is one of the classy examples for best use of life style. He has created wealth for Tata group and reputation. He has created millions of jobs across the globe and he works for others to get a better life style.

Negative ideas& plans within the individual = Bad life style = Real life negative hero.

So guys be positive in nature, it will give us fruitful results for lifetime.

There is no rich or poor, all are in our minds, all are one and all are alike. So let's work together, first improve ourselves & change others and help all who come to us. God sends them to test how you are and plans to give you super powers every day. On screen Krrish - Hrithik Roshan, the super star of Bollywood - the real Indian super hero was a true hero for his father Rakesh Roshan. He worked hard to make his father's project - Krrish Series come true. Result was super success.

Indians watched his super powers on screen and everyone was very happy. This is life style management, all powers, cash, gyaan was used in a proper way.

You will not believe this, every day we get energy, not from food which we have, but you and me get it from God. Energy is all the same for each one of us. It is up to us to utilize & perform like a true rock star.

Good Ideas + Positive Plans + Good habits + Game Plan + Good Diet + Willingness to help others on this planet + Good use of Gyaan = Healthy Smiley Life Style.

5 Stress Management

STRESS is every where and for everyone. One cannot avoid stress, it is how we manage it and control it. Stress can cause large or small damages, if not rectified at the right time. Stress can be either positive or negative.

If you work for others you get positive stress, that is good for our health,& if you work for yourself& only for yourself, then you get negative stress, bad for our health.

If stress is used in the right way, we can do wonders for society. Think and have stress for contribution to our country - India. For so many years, India has given us so much to us. It's right time for us to give back something in return and be useful. Your sweet little changes, developments and contributions can bring a New India.

Students across the world have stress, when they prepare for their exams. Some take it as a negative stress then result is failure, and some students take it as positive stress = rank holders. Hence, whenever we get stress factor, be calm, analyze the situation which we are in and then react, plan otherwise its harmful.

Practical Example: Salesman - If perceived sales targets as stress.

Positive Stress : Salesman = You end up planning and achieving your sales targets and you may even get best salesman of the year award.

Negative Stress : Confusion, health problems, losing interest in the job, accidents, no planning, may even lose the job.

Stress is for everyone, everywhere across the world. It can come in any form, some can pay you rewards, some destroy you as well. So welcome stress, take it positively. Be calm, think, plan, act, meet a guru, ask God to give powers to help others, your Stress is Out = Smile on your face.

Have a smiley ball with you all day, look at it, it makes you stress free and happy - so be like smiley balls, I am sure you will be happy all day.

6   How to be a Good Speaker & Improve Your Communication Skills.

LIFE is a theatre, so join theatre classes. This is a right place where a individual learns the art of speaking, it comes out naturally. You will be involved in different scripts and you act accordingly. You speak continuously in plays. The beauty of theatre classes is you will also lose fear factor within yourself& you will be extremely strong and confident& you will get a new person within you.

I have improved my communication skills by speaking to different class of people, animals, birds, trees, and all living beings on this planet, & also to some stars at night.

First I consider all are same and equal. I have spoken to drivers, cleaners, servers, CEOs of companies, young entrepreneurs, advertisers, carpenters, doctors, engineers, lawyers, actors, celebrities, politicians, teachers, gurus, construction workers, factory workers, vegetable vendors, super market owners and staff members, hyper market staff, different business school students,& to my students at MSRCASC. I want everyone to have top communication skills, so that we all can raise our voice in public for good changes in society.

Practical's: Mirror Approach & Speak with everyone

1. Mirror is your best friend, take a dozen of live topics and start speaking in front a mirror. Practice this activity everyday fifteen minutes till you are confident.

2. Speak to your friends, water, birds, animals, stars, general public.

3. Make new friends; speak to them as though you know them from many years. In the process you learn more, your knowledge bank will grow.

If everyone practice all these for say 100 days, then you will be the most powerful communicators. All the Best.

7 Marketing Management - Tap the Market Before Someone Does

MARKETING means making products and services available in the hands of the consumer at the right second, our efforts should be much faster than our competitors in the market. All efforts will bring in high profits, hence we need to tap the market with our products and services before our competitors, this will fetch us competitive advantage in the market place and also we can connect with our consumer well, making consumer inform about the products and services offered by a company is the prime objective of marketing, and the rest follows. If one loses he does not make any money and all the hard work which is put in goes waste, So set your marketing actions right. We need to know the following in Marketing, for handling any product or service to a end consumer:

1. Know your consumer habits & taste.

2. Know your competition.

3. Know your present market share & see how to increase your market share.

4. Plan your sales & after sales service.

5. Pricing - Today we have competition from all sides, so pricing should be in such a way that it should be acceptable to our end consumer.

6. Channel of distribution - Factory - C&FA - RS Points - Wholesalers - Retailers and it varies from company to company.

7. Hire the right sales force - Hire only who are dedicated and who likes to make a sales career in the respective sector.

8. Plan your advertising and sales promotion in a planned manner, so that it will give us results.

9. Supply Chain Management: should be in order, because customer will not wait for us, so timely delivery to our dealers are a must, making products and services available 24/7 will get more sales & you also get happy and loyal customers.

10. Training is a must - Communicate your goals to your sales staff regularly, customize your training materials so that there is a win - win situation, so that your sales staff, will achieve it for the company and for themselves.

11. Rewarding the sales team: Our Bread and butter comes from our customers, and our sales force is actively responsible for all the sales happening within the business, we need to take great care of our sales force like our children and ensure that they are happy with all the compensation given to them and also ensure facilities are adequate and for super performers reward and promote.

12. Assign the Sales Force to their respective areas by doing a beat plan regularly.

13. International Marketing - we do promotion, we participate in exhibition, take local government and embassy support, set up

factories, get license to operate and to do business globally, hiring staff. The basic is always the same even in International marketing.

Today Marketing needs human touch & unique concepts and strategies in order to survive in a highly competitive market.

Practicals: The Tea Shop (Chai Adda) Let us say we want to open a Tea Shop (Chai Adda), what all we need let us list first:

Experience of the industry, current market trends, choosing a budget for our store, choosing a brand name, selecting an area to operate, furniture, branding materials, interiors, exterior designs, computers, business registrations with local corporations and most important sales staff. Hire the best, be unique, catch the attention of youth. Food menu should be in such a way that people should come back. And we need to do local print ads in newspapers, banners, college events sponsors, etc. And if the store is doing well, multiply the number of outlets and you can even make franchisees, then your business rocks.

Marketing is not all about selling more or to inform about the products and services. Marketing also helps one to organize things effectively, there by a firm makes more profits.

Marketing makes you think & act & it brings more incoming money. We utilize all the firm resources to best of our abilities; that's marketing management.

8 Fast Moving Consumer Durables Sector (FMCD)

Fast Moving Consumer Durables Sector (FMCD) - Daily needs appliances for domestic purposes and luxury products, like television, a big fat box now comes as a LCD Tv, Refrigeration products for both hotels & homes, air conditioning products, micro ovens, washing machines, induction stoves, kettles, toasters, grinders, mobile phones, DVD players, watches and jewellery also comes under FMCD industry. All most all have 3 year life span, except jewellery, then the customer goes for new innovative products from the industry.

TTK Prestige, Hawkins, Bajaj, Samsung, Titan Industries Limited, Voltas, IFB, LG, Sony, Whirlpool, Blue Star, Videocon, are some of the players in the FMCD segment.

Why is this Industry Attractive:

1. Rise in Disposable Income as everyone is working or doing business.

2. Consumer finance from major banks and the best part is loan is approved in five minutes. You could even take away your appliances on the go.

3. Rural market opening.

4. Many international and national players.

5. Wide range of products.

6. After sales service.

7. Factory seconds dealers

FMCD employs a large number of people today as cashiers, floor managers, managers, filed executives, service executives, finance executives, etc.

All these products are daily use products. If one does business or if one joins as an employee, I am sure one can make a lot of money and be happy and make others happy & most important you are giving comfort solution products to an end consumer, so as a customer he is happy. So please keep in mind - Human Touch Factor = More Sales.

Ask for the customer who drops in to your store, what is he looking for, and give suitable solutions. Be presentable, know your products, explain the benefits = more sales.

9   Moral Science: Mother Earth

IF we remember, we had moral science as one of the subjects in every standard. As this book is like a full time course in management, I have included few chapters on moral science with different topics.

Do we own a piece of land, site, villa, commercial land, residential land, farm land, holiday land? Answer to this question = NO.

Land owner is always Mother Earth. She is the right owner of the land.

Mother Earth is the actual owner of the land which we purchase. We never own this land, because it will be in white papers. So please make the right use of land, which we live in. For name sake our property documents will reflect our name in the papers, it keeps changing from person to person. We spend life time in acquiring land, which is not ours, so make the best use of the land.

Some standards we need to follow, with respect to land matters : Never go behind acquiring property. Please share your piece of land in case someone needs it i.e. give temporary accommodation or if your rich make them live with you, because in future there will be huge shortage especially in cities.

By practicing it, Mother Earth will be happy. Have a mantra in life - share - share - share - we will all live happily. Joy of giving and sharing with others is the ultimate satisfaction one can ever get.

Keep your Planet clean, plant more trees, love trees - good for our health.

Life is not all about how much one acquires but how much one gives

10 Indian Society - Indian Ethos and Values in Modern Management

INDIA has a huge population, more than 1 billion, growing on & on. More than 50% of the population is youth - young Indians. We have some of the oldest empires, Gupta period. We have mix religions, Hindus, Muslims, Christians, Sikhs, Buddhists, Jains, old people, family set-up & bonding, business men, traders, actors, sports stars, celebrities, educated class, best English speaking people. All have one thing in common - strong value system within themselves. Hence every individual worked for the family and for maximum contribution to the society. So we have great families, great business people, great educated class, great business empires were so strongly built that they rule even today.

Living Example : Tata Group - Even today, Tata group, its people, vendors, whoever are associated with the group focuses on enriching the quality of life of the people. They have Tata Tea and Tata Coffee - beverages, Tata Housing - best of its class homes for High class, Tata Nano for all classes. The company has products and services for everyone. The business function is good even today because they work for the people of India. Rest, they say profits come naturally. My Indian people, is the golden business principle followed by the Tata group. Hence even today it is one the topmost highly ethical and highly respected business houses in the country.

We have best land, farmers, technology, computers, BPO, KPO, information technology, zoos, parks, mountains, rivers, birds, animals, wild life, auto brands, variety of food products, schools, colleges, Indian Institute of management, Indian Institute of Technology, science, commerce, politics, beautiful men and women, Miss India, Mr India, 3 Khans of Bollywood, clothes, brands, malls, entertainment, music, dance, pubs, 5 star hotels, spa, websites, salons, coffee day chains, builders and developers, dealers, mobile, internet. We have everything in our country, we just need to ensure that value system remains the same for ever. So please be responsible for our India. The way we love our parents, relations, friends, brands, the same way one should love INDIA. We have experienced best food chains - good different types of food, best clothing brands, best housing facilities. We are taking so much from India, it is high time to bring in a new change in India. If each one of us does some new changes, then we can beat the rest of the world. So guys new change is from you. Future India is in your hands, wake up, transform and do something where the world says -

I love India & I love Indians.

11 Business Communication

COMMUNICATION plays a very important role in today's business. The best communicator brings name, fame and loads of incoming cash to his business enterprise. All business transactions happens if you communicate well with the customer, understand their needs and customize your talks.

Each one of us should have strong understanding of his business, industry, products or services, competitors, market trends, rules of business, customer tastes. This makes one easy to communicate well with the customer.

Communication with customer should have a human touch factor. Communication in business means best writing, good communication skills & transferring information.

Practical Example
If we go to a mall, we see best communicators as sales consultants. Each store has managers, sales consultants, all brands have good communicators. This way they present themselves and their communication skills are top class, this makes one buy more products and services.

Communication is a medium to transfer information for a purpose, so our purpose should be achieved.

Communication is cash, we spent lot of energy in transferring information to our customer, so it should not go waste.

Communication also helps an individual to get more knowledge, cash, contacts in industry. So guys what you waiting for, be best communicators.

12 Human Resource Management

RECRUITMENT of new staff, induction, training and development, retaining good staff members, motivating employees.

HRM revolves around people and ends around people. It's all about how to manage your employees, so that there will be a win-win situation for both the parties. So have a human touch principle. We respect our parents, gurus, elders, etc., the same care and affection we need to show towards our employees, then only we can expect the same love and care and results from our employees. Humans interact with humans in offices, so we need to respect each other and learn and achieve our organization's objectives.

If there is a problem, the solution is, have a human touch principle. Human knowledge and their skills should be mutually benefitted, keeping in mind our HRM Fun da.

Human resources are the most valuable assets in any organization. Hence first and foremost, we need to ensure that we get or hire the right people for the specific profiles. In India, there are lot of employment opportunities and talented people, gap is no right people to join.

Practical: HRM Any organization, profit making or nonprofit making, the main asset is always humans - talented skilled manpower. Before we hire someone, we need to have an inventory HR check plan; first we need to check what are the openings and what new business we may enter in the future, and hire accordingly. Talented people are in plenty waiting for you, so hunt down the right guy. Never hire an employee whose vision is changing all the time and who has no goals, or who is planning to join for a short term. Only hire someone who says 'I am interested' and who says 'I love your business model'. Most of the employees joining Tata group, even today join out of their trust in the Tata's. All talented people think that it a right place to be in for all their life. Most of the Tata employees who had joined in the old economy businesses have left the company only after retirement. That is the trust which Tata group has created in the market.

They look after the employees like a baby, induct, train, place, retrain, promote, reward regularly, assign new roles and responsibilities, foreign assignments. And the result is happy employees in Tata's. So make your employees responsible and share your vision and values.

13 Knowledge Management

Knowledge management is a process, where the entire organization and its people i.e. employees learn new gyyan. They also relearn a few things, implement and adapt to the new organization.

Any knowledge transfer of any material is useful to humans, so it is up to us to make the best use of it.

Knowledge is storing, capturing words, sentences, pictures, ideas, videos, subjects for future organization use.

It's not how much knowledge we store, but how we use it. All knowledge gained will be of a waste unless we put it into practice.

Many individuals, companies have been benefitted with the use of knowledge management. It brings best world-class business systems and practices.

So guys, knowledge management should be in such a way that it should bring in a new change in India. So you young business leaders, learn new things, implement them and adapt yourself to it and bring a new change to yourself, your company you work for and bring in new change in India.

This is the true meaning of Knowledge Management.

14 World of Beauty Salons

In olden days, we had barbers, where we used to go for a shave and a haircut for men and for ladies, most of it was a home natural care. Super rich class used to call a specialist at their homes and they used to get customized beauty solutions at their places. Now, it's different, we have many beauty clinics, parlors, salons, spas across India and some like Lakme Salon have stores in major cities.

Today if you spend a few thousand rupees, one can be the most good looking man and woman. All have customized beauty solutions and treatments.

Today if you want to be in a profession of beauty business, there are a lot of certification courses across India & making others beautiful is an art so it pays you as well. Celebrities spend heavily to look good, so it is one of the fastest growing service business.

All you need is to open your store, brand it, hire professionals, do aggressive marketing, give a customer a new feeling, make them look beautiful, then you make lot of money.

15 A for Aim and A for Archery

Each one of us should have a target, so we need focus. Hence archery practice improves concentration levels. If you start practicing it, it will give you immense happiness. It will build a new direction in our lives. Archery does not build negatively but a person improves his way of life. There will be total transformation within individuals. Archery is a traditional practice in India. It was mastered by Rama, Arjuna, Karna, Abhimanyu, Parasurama. Kings and many others used it in the forest, made bows and arrows for hunting or for war.

Many foreign nationals still practice archery every day to get the right focus factor.

Have a Archery practice once a week or everyday. See the results within yourself.

Love archery to hit the bulls eye - the bulls eye is your targets in life. Any target or material goal should be indirectly benefiting for the society.

16 Summer Project

SUMMER Project - Live practical exposure of business problems in a given company. Students have to do a project, identify a problem and have to give solutions for the same.

Top business schools, universities have interviews to do a summer project. Many companies come to colleges and pick the best business students to do project works. Most of the students get paid to do a summer project work.

Our parents have dreamt about good future for us. So it is our responsibility to make their dreams come true. So summer projects are very important, choosing a company, industry usually decides your future, because most of the summer interns have been offered jobs in the same company with good package.

Summer projects are a learning tool and a practical challenge to prove our metal. So guys this is very important task of your life - summer projects for some has changed their lives. Most of the students who have opted for Hindustan Unilever Limited, Nestle, Tata group of companies, Reliance, Aditya Birla Group, KPO companies, ICICI, HDFC, HSBC, Advertising agencies, Investment banking companies in their summer project work have got pre-placement offers from these companies. So we have to take our summer project work very seriously.

So when we start a summer project, we should learn about the company, products, group, organization structure, goals, vision and mission, turnover, competitors, market trends, market share, market moves, almost everything. Then decide on a topic of your choice or if the company has assigned you a project, work towards the same lines, as per companies instructions. Keep informed about each and every progress about your summer project work to company mentor and college guide.

All project work has to be done with special care, because someone out there is ready to offer you a good job with good package. Please take guidance of company mentor and college guide or your professor and follow the reporting rules.

17 Organization Study

Some of the university students who are pursuing their MBA program, have organization study as part of their curriculum.

Organization study is a right and a very good practical learning method for students to know about various industries and their companies in India.

First make a decision that you want to pursue your career in finance, marketing, systems, human resource, production, etc., before you even join an MBA program.

Decide your sector that you will work in the future - Automobile, Telecom, Financial Organizations, CA Firms, FMCD, FMCG, Retail. Decide and make a list of your companies you like to work with, do not go behind brand names & top companies. Even start-up firms give huge learning and earning opportunities.

Do projects as per University rules.

By the end of the your project, one should know the history of the company, when did they start the organization and with what capital. Organization structure, product or services, turnover, goals and objectives, vision and mission statements of the company, manpower, total size of business, departments like HR, Marketing, Systems, Finance, Law, R&D, Administration. If our behavior and attitude is good, you may even get an opportunity to work with the company where you do your organization project work, so please take it seriously.

Kindly take full support of your Gurus, seniors, relatives, friends, company staff, no one will stop you from learning. So guys capture data in your minds for future use.

18 Out of Home consumption - The Food Business

Out of home consumption is on the rise in India. As many educated graduates passed out from their colleges, jobs were in plenty in India across different industries, people were very busy and had no time to cook, hence we found out of home consumption in India. We found that youth, college buddies, school buddies, adults, senior citizens all like to have food outside. Trends have changed from traditional eating inside the home to eating outside. Hence there is lot of food business opportunity today. We find food in streets - road side vendors making mouthwatering dishes at affordable prices, hang out cafes, ice cream zones, exclusive food chains and bar and restaurants, many tiffin rooms, many south indian darshinis, fast food hubs, food courts with multi food brands all operating under one roof, pubs, big star hotels, big food menus and unlimited food. We have KFC, McDonald's, Barista, Coffee day, South & North Indian Restaurants, Bengali, Thai, Western, Continental, Coorg food lovers, Punjabi High end restaurants. They all serve us best tasty idli, vada, dosa, maddur vada, uddina vada, masala dosa, rava dosa, ragi dosa, plain dosa, paper dosa, kesai bhath, upma, puliyogare, pongal, vangibath, vegetable bonda, chaats, masala puri, sev puri, pani puri, bonda soup, bajji's, thaali's, rajma masala dal fry, jeera rice, plain rice, veg paulav, veg mix curry, palak curry, chinese food like noodles, fried rice, chicken lollipops, pasta, burger, salads, samosa, chicken rolls, veg rolls, dam biryani, kebabs, fish curry, fish masala, boneless fish, kerala & mangalore fish varities, kheema ball, kheema masala, chaapati, raggi balls, nann, roti, butter rotis, chulcha, biryani rice, egg masala, egg pakoda, lassi, tea, coffee, andra style food, chilli and spicy food varities, hyderabadi meat dishes, mumbai vada pav, rasgulla, carrot halwa, kulfi, badami sweets, ladoos, mysooru pak, grape juice, naril pani, beer, vodka, whisky, cockails, mockails, fresh fruit juices, cane juices, bihari food, kashmiri, french, fusion, italian, japanese, mexican, barbeque.

Mouth watering isn't it, we have a ocean of varieties of food in India, all are food lovers, hence being in food business is one of the most profitable& novel business, because giving food to others on this planet is fun and it will also gives you great satisfaction, and off course if you do well, lots of incoming cash, so make a good food business plan, learn the art of cooking, do market surveys, Do a SWOT analysis, name your business, register your business, promote your business, make food with love and special care, if we prepare food with love, then the rest will be the history.

Today in small food business, business owners make easily $ 1000 per month as profits. So industry has big players, be different in your approach, we do not sell food we satisfy your hunger. So please give Indian masses unlimited food at affordable prices, that should be your business mantra.

19 Shelter Business - The Real Estate

TATA housing, DLF, Oberoi Reality, Godrej, Pride, Bren, Mantri, HM group, Nikoo Homes, Krishna Shelton. 1000 + major big builders and developers across the country are giving us new homes and a new India, with the list increasing every day. In olden days, we had plenty of space. Our great grand pas used to buy or inherit 100 acres of land and there were called as land lords. Gone are the days, now as we enter into fast developing mega cities, we find a lot of people entering cities for employment or to pursue their interest and academics. We have even foreign visitors and investors. India is a place everyone likes to settle down, to live in this beautiful country. So we now have shortage of prime land or properties. It is very difficult to own an independent land to build a home inside the heart of a city is very expensive. It is houseful, option is outskirts of the city. Lot of developers are giving birth to their new unique homes, plots, sites, villas, flats, commercial properties. Hence we also have infrastructure companies to support them.

So, now people live in big and luxurious apartments. In every city we have huge requirement of talented manpower. So guys if you want to be in shelter business there is big business that at the same time you are making someone's dreams come true, that's their dream home. There are lot of builders and developers waiting for you. All you need is a minimum graduation or masters, market knowledge, interest in shelter business, land prices gyaan, registration formalities, how to read a document, khata and paper works & if you have money you could even be a entrepreneur. This is not all. It will definitely pay you a lot of money and guarantee you own space for yourself on this beautiful planet.

There are also various other manpower requirements in this business like Human resource, Marketing, Sales, Agents, Admin, Security, Construction Workers, Architects, Legal,Purchase, Interior Designers.

This business is non stop 24/7 industry.

It works round the year, 365 days, because if we complete one project and sell, new project work is in place & is on and on. If you are a beginner, you can earn any where between 15 k to 20 k and then there is no limit to your income. Plant more green along with your construction activities.

20 Psychology

God has made all human beings different, different in shape, color, ideas, views, upbringing, goals, strategies, mindsets. Everyone heads towards different lives - some take life positively and some choose negative life. Negativety leads to destruction and only destruction, so choose the path of positive life. We have to learn from many negative personalities, they have destroyed themselves and others. There ideologies in life were crazy, examples : demons like mahisasura, duryodhana and many others. If they would have taken their lives positively they would have been super heroes like Krissh, hence choosing good life and good paths is in our own hands. We have more than 50 management subjects, what do we learn from them. All prepare us to be super heroes and not demons. So we need to make the best use of our management subjects and make it useful for others on this planet. By doing this, we get promotions in our company which we work for and we also contribute to our Indian economy. India is rich in culture and its talented humans. So we need to make the best use of this. Hence any Indian company or a foreign company should first make a good selection of its manpower, hire as per the job requirements. Please hire who is interested and who is dedicated. Dedication of the employees is shown in first few weeks or months. Companies want super heroes and not demons, observe employees behavior, have a close watch on them. Because their actions can bring in positive or negative changes in the company. If there actions are positive it's healthy for the company. And if their actions are negative then it's a concern for the company. So sit with the employees, understand their needs and counsel them if necessary and give them a chance and make them work again.

Psychology - human beings are so different, each one of us is different the way we walk, dress, learn, reactions, education, hobbies, ideas, contribution, memories, lot of things are much different. Each one of us would have been the same if our religion, caste, creed, color, ideas, and most important our upbringing was the same. Now all of us can start a new beginning; no matter what we have learnt, our past, age, if one decides, we all can make large difference within ourselves and for others and we can also contribute maximum to which ever company or organization we work for & we should ensure one thing, we should not cause damages to others. Human Psychology + ve = Good for the organization and for the individual = High Growth in Life.

Positive traits = more and more rupiahs and you stay healthy and happy and others feel nice to approach you.

All are different in our approach, tastes and preferences of the individuals are changing day by day. One's behavior affects another person, their mindsets and their actions will have to be studied. We call it as 'what's on your mind is what you deliver', you deliver positive energy or negative energy.

The best way to know our own psychology is simple, close your eyes, remember your past, check your positive and negative work. Not too late guys, every day till your last breath is your new day so do positives.

21 Automobile Industry

MARUTI Suzuki, Tata Motors, General Motors, Hero Motor Corp, TVS Motors, Tafe, Ford, Hyundai, Toyota, Renault, Mitsubishi, Nissan, BMW, Hindustan Motors, Skoda, Volkswagen, Mercedes Benz, Force Motors, Jaguar Cars, Land Rover, Audi, Fiat, DC Design Auto, Volvo, Bharat Earth Movers Limited, Eicher Motors, Bajaj, Vespa, KTM Sports Motorcycles, Mahindra & Mahindra, Ashok Leyland, Piaggio, Honda Cars Limited, Yamaha Motors, Caterpillar Inc, JCB.

The list is endless, so many auto companies and their various brands operating in the country. We see the industry is growing rapidly and at fast pace, as there are many car and bike lovers in the country. Hence production at all their factories are on the rise. It employs a large manpower for all their functional areas like production, marketing, sales, human resource, finance, security, administration, after sales service, systems. All the companies have a strong network of dealers spread across the country. All you need, if you guys want to join production is diploma in automobiles, or auto designer like DC, or bachelors in automobile engineering then there are jobs waiting for you & if you want to join marketing and sales, all you need is a minimum of graduation or MBA. So guys know your brand, company, car and bike completely. Give top class presentation about your cars and bikes to prospective customers. The more you guys sell units, the more you get paid in the form of incentives. It is a highly paid industry for top performers, many companies, many brands, huge profits, huge opportunities in automobiles sectors.

Entry level sales job is a Sales Consultant :

Job Profile: Selling the car and bike to prospective customers, to both showroom customers and generating leads from field activities in the market.

1. Know your company

2. Know your job

3. Know your industry and competitors

4. Know your competitors' pricing

5. Know you car/ bike/tractors/commercial vehicles/ATVs/etc.

6. Practice your sales technique many times with your seniors till you be perfect

7. Know you car and bike auto machine parts

8. Know pricing of different brands

9. Know availability of cars and bikes for faster deliveries

10. Know RTO registration formalities

11. Prepare yourself well in advance for payment follow-ups and customer deliveries

Regular training, follow-ups, love and care towards employees makes a auto dealer sell more units. Organize birthday parties, festival celebrations, regular health check-ups, canteen facilities, parties, regular rewards for top performers, cash payouts, good minimum salary. The more you pay cash and show special concern towards your employees, the more they get motivated and remain loyal and work hard and show results.

So guys what are you waiting for, huge earning potential industry, so go auto selling.

Happy Cars and Bikes

22 Insurance Industry

INSURANCE industry is one of the biggest industries employing millions of people in India. It has both government and private players. Foreign Direct Investment has gone up. IRDA controls all the insurance business in India. They lay mapping and provide rules and regulations within which an insurance company has to operate - starting from licensing to approving of the products. It also protects the customers of various policy holders of different insurance companies. Employment is huge in this industry, one can start as a relationship manager or as a sales manager in insurance and can go up to be a CEO. You can even sell insurance products to customers directly or you can make insurance agents under you and make them sell. As an agent or an advisor of any insurance company, one can make a decent amount of money in this trade. One should have excellent contacts in the market, then training is given by the respective insurance companies, then you have to pass an IRDA - Insurance Regulatory and Development Authority Test. Then you will be given a unique insurance advisor code, then you can start selling in the market. If your customer buys a insurance product from you, then you will make huge commission, generally 20-30 percent varies from product to product. That is really big money, without any investment in business, for all that you need is dedication, hard work, disciplined approach to sell insurance products. The best part is you could work part-time or full-time depending on your convenience.

Some Insurance companies in India: LIC, ICICI Prudential, Reliance Life, Bajaj Allianz, Birla Sun Life, SBI Life, Max Life, HDFC Standard Life, Tata AIG, ING Vysya Life

23 Banking Industry

SBI, State Bank of India is the country's oldest and number one bank in India. We have today, both private and government and co-operative banks spread across India. Today banking is so easy, convenient and fast, as we have internet banking, mobile banking, electronic fund transfers, ATMs. We can even choose our favorite account number, relationship banking, NRI banking, High Net worth Accounts. We have even foreign players like Deutsche Bank, HSBC, Citi bank. Banking industry employs a large number of educated, experienced people, they have jobs in IT, HR, Sales, Marketing, Recovery, Legal, Administration, Security, Training and Development, Finance, Cashiers, Helpers, House keeping. So one has to be dedicated and customer oriented. You can join banking from 8 am to 8 pm. So guys if you have the skillset and interest in banking, go ahead and join banking industry. Plenty of jobs, both direct and indirect jobs (DSA) with the banks.

Banking is very simple, you put your hard earned money in a safe place, you need a saving bank account for yourself, then you may need a cheque book, ATM debit card. You may also need a credit card, auto, home loans, personal Loans, business loans. You can even keep your documents and gold and precious items in safe lockers, you can even lock your investments in fixed deposits and recurring deposits. You can even open a demat account for trading in stock market with special assistance from banks. Hence banks are one stop place for all your financial requirements. So guys banks today are more or less like an FMCG, everyone contacts a bank for some or the other reasons, so there is huge earning and learning potential in the banking industry.

We have HSBC, Deutsche Bank, Bank of America, Axis Bank, HDCF Bank, Yes Bank, JP Morgan Chase, IDBI, ICICI, Jammu and Kashmir Bank, Bank of Nora Scotia, bank of Maharastra, Ratnakar Bank, Bank of Borda, Indus Bank, Bank of Tokyo, SBI, plenty of banks to choose for all your requirements.

Happy Banking

24 Jewellery Business

TANISHQ - the jewellery store from Titan Industries Limited, Nakshatra, D'dmas, Nirvana Gold and Diamond jewellery, Gili, Asmi Diamond Jewelry, Orra, Sangini, Malabar Gold and jewellery. So many brands are operating in India, offering unique traditional and modern designs to Indian masses and the market is growing. Gold is also treated as an investment during emergencies in India, so many buyers. There are also golden harvest schemes, where you keep saving some money for future purchase of gold jewellery. Jewellery business in India has created a lot of employment opportunities. They offer jobs in areas of designing, merchandising, store design, interior design, sales staff, human resource, administration, marketing; security is the top most priority in jewellery business in India. You never know Dhoom Dhoom Bikers may drop in any time. So this is one of the best industries to work for. In olden days, we used to depend upon our goldsmith to do all the house hold jewellery, super rich class & queens used to call the best goldsmith & best jewellery designers to their homes and ask them to show a lot of designs and then order gold, silver, diamonds on the spot. Even today top jewellery brands have home visits for super rich class, high net worth individuals and celebrities.

All you need is great interest in this industry and go ahead there are jobs waiting in this industry.

25 ITES Industry

Business Process Outsourcing (BPO), BPO is a system of business, where a part of your business like customer care, finance, technological support, data entry, medical transcriptions, billing, maintenance is done by others and is outsourced to an another country. Labor is expensive in other countries, most of the citizens in other countries depend on customer care, to give complaints or to get solutions, it can be for placing a order to buy a product or a service or to give complaints or to know a specific information. Manpower is expensive in most of the super developed countries, so they all found a solution, that is outsource. They made their back office operations in India, because number one - we have good English speaking people and good communicators, second - labor is not expensive. Thanks to many countries who have created millions of jobs for Indians. Reason is simple as discussed earlier, we have quality, trained good English speaking citizens. This industry has created a lot of job openings, but for sure, we have done justice till date. BPO industry has contributed a lot to the nation's economy. They have operations in big metros in India. We have companies like HCL, Wipro, Infosys TCS, and much larger players, competition is also slowly picking up from other countries. Overall working in a BPO Industry is changelling, fun, and lots of cash incentives.

Hence in this industry one gets fun, satisfaction, music, dance, transport facilities, good salary, incentives, good culture, outings, ethics, yoga, gaming, gym facilities, growth, learning, promotions, training, growth opportunities, good food, learning. So guys BPO Industry Rocks.

One can start as an agent, then you can climb the ladder till the CEO-Operations in the same company. It is a great place to be, because you get new friends, new talents, fun, one can make a lot of money as incentives daily. If one works non-stop for 10 years, your bank balances will grow.

26 Hospital Management

Fortis, Apollo, Manipal, Nimhans, Narayana Hrudayala, Hosmat, Columbia Asia, Sagar Hospital, Mallya Hospital, Vikram Hospital. So many hospital brands, today & its increasing on a daily basis across the country. India has seen a tremendous change in the hospital-health care industry. My special thanks to health care machine manufacturers, pharmaceutical industry, highly experienced doctors from different specializations, best nurses who give special care with love and affection, and to all those who so ever related to hospital-health care industry. Let us take today, a practical living God of heart surgery in India, Shri Dr. Devi Prasad Shetty, Chairman Narayana Health, such a novel doctor, who masters the art of heart operations. He saw that majority of people from India and abroad are suffering from heart related issues, hence he made Narayana Health, Bangalore.

Dr. Devi Prasad Shetty, I truly respect this great man. He is a God to millions of people who approach him, and he says we will take care, the best use of medical knowledge - the living God in the health care industry.

Narayana Health is also a temple for millions of people, who get their heart treatment done. They have a lot of in-patients, so more patients walk-in every day with their problems. Narayana Health gives treatments at affordable prices, people fly from different countries to get cured. They have best quality treatments, procedures, skilled doctors and machines and they have a human touch approach towards their patients. Doctors are well-paid in Narayana Health, they have some rich donors who sponsor for the needy poor man's operations, a good cause in society is supported by everyone. All staff at Narayana Heath is well trained, they know their daily task, there are busy, yet they will ensure the given task is completed. All the staff is working in Narayana Health not for money, but for people, for us to get the best health care (the writing of Narayana Health was from my direct visit to Narayana Health). 'I will cure attitude' should be there at hospitals, the rest will follow. You should not send any patient back, due to money or some other reasons, that's health care management, that's hospital management according to me.

Thanks to the government, now we have sanjeevini health care cards, health insurance cards, that is cashless facility up to certain limit.

Some hospitals are like 3 Star and 5 Star hotels, fully loaded with all the luxuries.

All hospitals have openings in all the departments like HR, Finance, Systems, Marketing& Sales, Purchase, Administration, Security, Nurses, Doctors, lots of employment and the best part is you make others happy and make them mentally free. It's a novel trade to be in, all you need is 'I will cure attitude' then this is the best place to work.

27 Hotel Management

Taj Vivanta, ITC Windsor, Taj West end, ITC Royal Gardenia, The Leela Palace Kempinski, The Lalit Ashok, The Oberoi, The Golden Spa & Hotel, The Keys Hotel, The Laitha Mahal Palace - Mysore. So many hotel brands are operating today in India, there is a huge employment opportunity in this sector. Hotel Industry today, employs a large number of manpower for their daily requirements for their various operations like Human Resource, Marketing& Sales, IT, Finance, Cashiers, Billing Executives, Purchase, Housekeeping, Security, Managers, CEO, GM.

Today we see one of the finest hotels across India, we have lodges system, bed systems at the lower end, at the higher end we have 3 star, 5 star, and luxury hotels. Almost everyone offers best class food and room service, there are also serviced apartments like hotels today and they are growing in numbers in India, serviced apartment are loaded with full luxury.

Most of the hotels offer best food like Indian, Chinese, Continental, Andhra type, Punjabi, Mexican. All best food under one roof, some customers drop in to these stars hotel only for the food, their varieties of dishes are mouth watering and very tasty. All food which is prepared with love and care, is what a customer expects. So managing a hotel is not all that easy today, great care has to be taken to maintain the quality of food and service levels in any hotel.

We have some of the best architectural designs in the hotels like one of the hotel called Keys in Hosur road, Bangalore - the hotel structure from outside looks like a key.

So many 3 star, 5star, lodges, home stay, jungle lodges, boat houses, serviced apartments, spas, etc. business is huge in this industry. So we have a course at graduate level as Hotel Management, where one learns the art of cooking and they also teach you how to manage a hotel.

So guys get ready to step into the world of hotel business, making guests happy is fun and exciting, and of course a lot of incoming cash.

28 Customer Relationship Management

MANAGEMENT of a customer is the top most priority in today's business. Customer is very choosy as their awareness level have gone up. They have information of all branded products and services at their finger tips, as all mobile phones are equipped with internet facility, access to information is easy at their go. So handling customers is not easy in today competitive situations in India. So in order to keep pace, we need to win the heart of our customers, we need human touch approach and good relationship with all customers every day. No customer is a waste of time, all customers can be mutually beneficial in some or the other way to our business. In India, we have places where customer likes to go back to same old hubs like MTR - Lalbagh road Bangalore, GTR Chamundipuram - Mysore, Oberoi Hotel. Many shops at Commercial Street and Brigade Road in Bangalore have same loyal customers at their street, reason is the new unique products and shop keepers selling quality products at affordable prices. Even after the malls have come around, Commercial Street and Brigade Road sales have not dropped much in these two streets, the reason is good sales and service to customers. It's even today's Bangaloreans favorite fashion shopping addas.

CRM is like handling accounts, we should ensure that our customer are an active account all the time.

CRM Example:

Case: FMCG Outlet - Super Market

If you go to a super market and buy all the necessary groceries and household items for yourself, this super market is good, cool. New products are added every month, i.e. you find something new every time you come back to the super market to shop. The place is also happening, they also serve free goodies every time you shop with them and the super market guys have made you satisfied, all products are clean, new stock is added every week. They also give you cash discounts for bulk shopping. They even do home delivery, so this customer account is called Customer No 1 = Account No 1 = Mr Kumar. Mr Kumar is very happy with this super market and is always loyal to this super market only and ensures that he buys and also refers his friends and relatives to this super market. By this more and more accounts are added and there will be more incoming cash to your business, this is CRM.

29 Industrial Relations

INDUSTRY is a group of people with different skillsets. Domain experience comes together with capital, labor, business plans and ideas, to achieve a common goal for the firm or an enterprise, thereby all contribute to the country's development.

In order to make our given industry successful, it can be any industry which we operate, we need to be united and have good industrial relations. As far as I have seen Tata group operate their factories with multiple locations across India, they have used land, water, resources and manpower to make best quality products. They have also given back to society in the form of employment. They have created large employment opportunities in India. Every employee is proud to work for Tata Group because they have taken care of employees so well, they treat them like their own family members, hence the result is no major fights among workers at Tata's. All employees have been assigned a task which they are committed to and will work towards it, and the rest the company is there to take care. They will be rewarded with incentives and promotions, this is a classical example of how to operate a business in India or aboard.

Industrial dispute may arise from some small confusions, rumors, or a purposeful action either by employee or employer. Employees who work for us, are working hard for us, they have expectations from us, it's the duty of the management to fulfill the same. Do not think twice, give more benefits and rewards to your employees. The more the employee stays loyal, the more he works hard and shows you results, which in turn brings in lots of incoming cash into the business. Any organization or factory first is its people, who work for them, no matter who they are and which class of society they belong to, we need to treat everyone with great care and we need to respect their work and reward them regularly.

Trade unions is a group of employees coming together and forming a union. There will be a union head or a leader. In today's environment salary alone is not enough for everyone to maintain our daily needs and aspirations. We need bonus and other incentives to take care of our other needs. Hence if a factory is doing well and making lot of profits and the management is not sharing wealth with the factory workers, then the Trade union comes into picture. Now they are active, all the workers complain that they are working hard and they need bonus & incentives. Then the trade union head will sit with the management and try to solve the issue. Issues sometimes can be for basic facilities like transport, food, work environment, medical insurance, leaves, children education.

A worker and the trade unions can fight for any issues, but one thing we need to understand is that our bread and butter is coming from our factory, so before one approaches the trade union, please keep one thing in mind, management can pay the workers if the factory is doing well, if they are making profits. If they are making loss, then all the factory workers should work hard day and night, bring positive changes in the factory and then demand for bonus. In today's age running a factory is not all that easy.

Do not go for strikes unless required. Reason is that management does not lose anything but it is the workers who lose their daily wages and other benefits. But if it is a worst situation then one has no choice, but nothing like sitting face to face and resorting the issue.

Performance based pay motivates a worker, so make extra production payments at regular intervals, i.e. produce more and earn more, same like sales, sells more and earn more. Here a worker produces more number of units per day and at the end of the week he gets extra cash payments. If this approach is adopted at any factory level across, both management and worker make a lot of money and in this case both are happy.

Any industrial program should contain : Top management support at all times, sound personal policies, regular training to employees, feedback of employees, suggestion to improve the organization. Most of the top management heads think that the answer the improve the organization lies in board meetings with top qualified people. But the right man is the worker, if we involve our workers, supervisors, and key managers in the board meetings, I am very sure that they can bring in positive changes in the organizations.

Industrial relations revolve around industry or a sector which we operate in. We need to maintain a healthy business climate both inside and outside our work places. Lots of people are inter-connected like train bogies in our business - employees, government, law and order, rules, deadlines, targets, business plan. At the end of the day, for any business the heart and soul is their employees, we need to ensure that they are happy. By this, any organization can earn a lot of money and also achieve good status in the market.

30 Service Management

INDIA is a land of rich resources - people, population, cultures, music, education, money, cricket, gold, silver, precious metals, food, land of tradition, rich value based system at homes, dance, travel, 50% of the population is youth, educated country men and women, styles, fashion, great minds, lovely people. We have the best institutes in India namely CFTRI (Central Food Research Institute - Mysore City), Indian Institute of Management (IIMs), Indian Institute of Technology (IITs), National Institute of Fashion Technology (NIFT). We have the best companies, Tata's, Birla's, Reliance, Oberoi.

India is young and growing every day, and it's a land of opportunities for millions. Best place to be on this planet is India. We have services in our every day life namely : Agriculture, Forestry& Fishing, Telecom, Mining and Querying, Manufacturing, Water and Electricity, Construction, Transport and Hotel, Finance& Insurance, Banking, one can get into service business sector as there is huge opportunities.

Service Sector can be classified as : Hospitality - Café, Hangouts, Hotels, Motels, Serviced Apartments, Resorts & Spa, Home Stay, Catering and Restaurant, insurance, Tourism and Travels, Health Care and Hospital Management, Housing& Construction, Communication, Entertainment, Advertising, Banking, Transportation and Logistics, Theme and Amusement Parks, Leisure Activities, Legal

Agency, Maintenance, Security Agencies, Research and Development, Investment Advisors, Accounting and Tax services, Real Estate, Personnel Services, Retail and much more.

Service management is all about how to make our service level - the best, the best and efficient to our customers. First we need to decide the nature of service business, then making a business plan, and making it work is the most important thing in today's business. Because customers will not come back if they have a bad experience from us. So customer service is the prime importance in any service business. Best service practical examples are : Mc Donald's, KFC, Café Coffee Day, Barista, MTR.

If you visit a McDonald's restaurant, it's a place with world wide presence, best interiors, best exteriors, clean & neat premises, best POPs, drinking water facility. All employees welcome guests who walk inside the outlet, all have uniforms, well presented, soft spoken, well dressed, smiling faces. They explain first about their food menu, then they take orders, then we get tasty bites in seconds, best world class service. This is what I call a best service level, there service level is top class.

If you take special care towards your customers, then if you follow human touch approach, then your services business can be seen from the sky. So customers are one who make our business grow bigger and bigger.

Happy Customer = Happy Service Business

31 Retail Management

RETAIL is a very big industry in India. It creates a lot of employment opportunities in India and abroad.

They are very famous retail giants like WalMart, Tesco, Metro Cash and Carry, Big Bazaar, Shopper Stop, Life Style, Food World, More Super Market & Hyper Market, Café Coffee Day, USPA, Mega Mart, Puma, Reebok, Nike, VIP, Spykar Jeans, Levis, Tata Star Bazaar.

This industry creates lots of revenues and also contributes to country's economic growth.

So retail is the best place to be in. There are also small and medium sized stores operating in India. Some sell clothes, ready to eat food items, groceries, plastic products, fashion articles, etc. Nature of business from brand to brand or from person to person varies in India.

Handling retail is not easy because they are lot of associated works which happen on a day to day basis (now let's take a clothing brand as an example)

A : Store Location: We need to ensure that our store is in right location, either in malls, high streets, or any busy areas. The store has to do well, so we have to find the best location for our store, examples are Commercial Street Bangalore, MG Road & Brigade Road Bangalore, Dev Raj Urs Road Mysore, Malls like Garuda Mall, Oasis Mall, Gopalan Mall, Total Mall, Mantri Mall Bangalore, Mall of Mysore. These are some places where the footfalls are high for any given brand as customers walk-in into these streets with an intention to buy goods. As rentals have gone up in all the major cities, one has to be very careful in choosing a right location.

B : Store Interiors: Gone are the days, where stores used to have simple lightings, simple furniture and fixtures. Now people walk into the store looking at the interiors. If it looks posh, then there are more advantages, more sales. So if you closely observe from the past 5 years, lot of foreign retail brands have entered into India, and there interiors look at their best and classy and flashy. Good interior works create good branding. Interior works have to be done with special care as lot of money goes into it. So we need to pay a lot of attention in making of a good store. Some works include wood work, lighting, flooring, air-conditioning, putting stickers, outside POP.

C : VM - Visual Merchandising - Once location and interior works are completed, now it's the work of VM guys to make the store look beautiful. VM works include display work both inside and outside the store. VM materials make the store look unique and cool. VM is the integral part of branding of the store.

VM works include:

1. Bringing related products which matches the store and the business profile

2. Stickers - Inside and Outside

3. Banners, Posters & Signage.

4. POP - Point of Purchase materials.

5. VM ensures all associated works will be meet as per the brand standards.

In big companies there is a separate department usually a team of 10 -15 people that takes cares of a brand or group of brands, VM works in the entire nation.

D : Stocks - It can be any brand or a product, stock keeping should be planned well in advanced so that we will not lose the sale and most important is, because of not keeping a particular stock in the store customer should not be disappointed. Hence there should be planning, we need to plan what sells best in our store. So order such stocks which are in demand. In apparel and organized retail formats, we have a person dedicated to do this job - Retail Planner. Retail Planner plans stocks for the entire season for all the stores in his region. He or she will also analyze what sells best at our store. So good co-operation is required from the store managers. Store manager is the face of the store so he has to give right data pertaining to the movement of stock in the store. All area sales managers, store managers, brand heads, logistics team, factory guys, store owners, all should be well-informed in advance about the movement of the stocks.

E : IT / Billing Machines - Once all these are set, we need IT tools and applications, computers, printers, fax machines, billing softwares, printer rolls, paper, stationery to run the store, we need to ensure all these are in the store.

F :Music & Good Speakers: Good Music at stores makes a customer's shopping experience fantastic. Customers love to come back and shop, if you have good collection of playing music. We should also display a certificate, issued from Indian performing rights society for playing music in the store.

G: Register your store and do regular auditing.

In apparel sector - there are two seasons, autumn winter and spring summer.
Presently we have self owned stores - small, medium, large outlets, franchisee outlets, multi brand outlets, hyper market, super markets, and company owned retail chains.
Some retail calculations which we will be helpful in running our store.

How many categories of products we have in our store? Last day sale, Last week total sales, our monthly, quarterly sale, yearly how much total sale has the store done? Total dispatches done from the warehouse to the store. What is the Current stock? Which stocks sell faster? Basket size - How many items we sell to one customer in one single bill? Total foot falls. Keep track of your store in all aspects, because we should ensure our store performs all the time.

For any store employing right people is a must. So employ like-minded people who like to make a career in retail. For guys out there, there are lot of job openings in security, store managers, fashion assistants, house keeping, maintenance, or you can start your own retail store. So guys get your business plans ready.

Happy Retailing

32 Self Defense

IN today's competitive environment we meet negative forces. Martial arts, karate and other self-defense techniques help us in taking care of ourselves, i.e. we can defend ourselves from negative forces and it helps us in danger.

They are multiple benefits in learning this art : we can protect ourselves from negative forces, we can train our minds, our minds will be in our control, we can strengthen our body, we get discipline in life, we will achieve our life's goals, we will improve physical performance, our body and mind stays active 24/7. We will improve our strength and stamina, our heart will be in best condition all the time, mind will be relaxed and cool. We will get a 'I will do it attitude in life', improve self confidence. Students do well in their exams, you love life and you start loving yourself. You will respect everyone in the society and most important society respects you. You will start bringing positive changes in the society.

Practical example is Mr Akshay Kumar from Bollywood. The Superstar has spent a lot of time in learning self defense. Akshay never asks one to fight in streets but his positive message is to be fit and powerful, so that one contributes in whatever manner to India.

33 Finance

ALL financial transactions has to be recorded, stored for future use either in our computers or in books.

Money plays a very important role in any business. If not managed well, it can make us upside down. So we need to have special care towards our money management.

Money does addition, subtraction, division and also multiplication, so if you only multiply your profits then your business card will have a new office address, the Moon. That's the power of multiplication.

Accounting is keeping financial records in the right place & in the right manner. These records will be useful to us and to others who have invested in our business.

There are professional accounting firms these days in the market. They handle from book keeping to auditing and also filing returns in commercial tax offices on a monthly and a annual basis. They also help us in giving right solutions from time to time.

So if you love money, then if you also like the art of recording things and money management, then it's the best place to be in. Financial knowledge helps in knowing where our business stands.

Every year we handle millions of transactions, so many incoming and outgoing cash transactions have to be recorded in one place. So recording of all these transactions is a must.

If you know financial basics, you will be highly paid in this industry. One has to dedicated as they are numbers involved in each financial transactions, lot of concentration is required to perform these tasks. There are huge openings in financial BPO and KPO, Finance Manager, Finance Assistant, Jobs in CA firms, etc. There is ofcourse a lot of money, people who are involved in finance trade will create a lot of wealth for themselves and for others.

34 Dance and Music

I cannot image a life without music and dance, playing musical instruments or listening to good music makes your mind fresh, cool, relaxing, entertaining, relieves stress. You will get confidence, you will love your life, you will make people happy around you, concentration levels improve, you will be patient, improved sleep quality, reduced fear and anxiety.

Some types of music are : Classical, Country, Electronic, Metal, Pop, Rap, Rock, Bollywood and Hollywood Music.

Half and hour per day listening to music or learning musical instruments makes one pure and fresh all day. One gets lots of energy directly from God, because even God likes music and dance.

When you dance you enter into a new world, your body and mind perform at it best, you stay pure and perfect.

Some types of dance : Disco, Folk Dance, Hip Hop, Jazz, Modern Dance, Step, Swing, Slow dance, Rumba, Quick Step, Ballet, Break Dance, Belly Dance, Cha-cha.

Benefits of Dance are : Purity in life, you get lots of energy. It makes you fit, makes you relax, gives peace of mind in life, builds strong bones, you will also burn calories, heart functioning will be at its best, healthy life style, entertainment to others. It reduces stress levels, will make you positive and thereby you can achieve your goals. You will love life and yourself.

35 Human Resource Consulting Business

KELLY services, Mafoi, Adecco, HR one are some of the top HR consulting business firms in India. India is a land of large talented workforce. Some get jobs through campus placements, relatives and friends, referrals and some get into government jobs. Not all are lucky so to fill the gap there are HR consulting firms these days. Getting jobs for people is one of the best and novel jobs one could do, helping getting a job or creating jobs for people is fun and highly rewarding. Indian market today needs the right man for the job, but there are very few right people, so it's the HR consulting firms who help companies to get the right people. HR consulting firms will first tie up with companies, will know what is their manpower requirements and then hunt for people in Naukri.com, Jobstreet.com, Timesjobs.com, Shine.com, etc. Then you will get a call from them, they will inform about various industries with different openings, then they take your updated resume, then they will send them for short listing to various company HR departments, then if shortlisted they will arrange for interviews, and next is selection and job offer. It is a huge business currently in India. One can get into HR consulting, by registing their business firm. You could even place people abroad, if you have good contacts. Having good contacts is a must for this business.

The best job every day is to get a job for others in the market.

36 Online Marketing

ONLINE marketing is creating a market place on the world wide web, i.e. on the internet. Online business is huge in India and is growing faster every day. Indians are highly knowledgeable, tech savvy, all use internet and mobile applications. In today's 24/7 work life, people do not find time to shop in the market place, so they want service providers. Hence in India, lot of young entrepreneurs came forward to capitalize on this big opportunity - Flipkart.com, snapdeal.com, yebhi.com, myntra.com.

Everyone has created their own unique websites, with lot of products and services. Today you can buy a product, order food, book your movie tickets, buy your travel tickets, you can even sell your products, all on the go.

First everyone makes people view their sites by posting their web address in other portals. Then they slowing start getting hits or clicks, from 100 to 10000, then from 10000 to one million clicks per day. Then through word of mouth and people who have purchased products online, customers start using more and more of such portals and buy more products every day. You can make your payments through debit and credit cards and you can also pay when the products are delivered at your homes or offices.

Flipkart.com is live practical example of how they utilized this big opportunity. Millions of products are sold every second worldwide.

So guys what are you waiting for, go ahead and start your own online business.

37 International Business

ALL firms, companies, manufacturing sector, banks and arts are going global. Flow of goods and services, cash, ideas, cultures, are going global. There are more options to buy for a consumer today. In international business, labor, capital, technology, movement is easy. It creates huge employment opportunities. Skilled manpower is the order of the day and is wanted across the globe. Around the globe transactions, every second someone is buying something in the world. So there are huge opportunities in manufacturing sector, new products and designs are being created every day across the globe.

There are different means of international business, namely export import trade, foreign direct investments, licensing, franchising, management contracts, tourism, etc.. In international business we get to produce more at the same cost i.e. there are more orders, more time, more production activities and cost of per unit comes down. Work more and earn more is the trend in international markets. Availability of international products and services is now made available in the market place.

Goal is to achieve maximum long term profit in our business transactions. Low cost per unit = maximum profits, this is achieved in international business. Value is created by different departments of every company in research and development, production, marketing and sales, service, materials management, human resource management, information systems. In international business, we utilize the services of talented like-minded manpower across the globe i.e. we hire talented skilled people who suit our business requirements and who bring value to our business. The important thing in international business is that you stay and operate close to raw materials i.e. you can set-up our factories nearer to raw material availability.

Some benefits of international business :Being global, Being largest producer, Being largest employer, Achieving a low cost per unit of production, Saving time and energy, Achieving economies of scale, Making high Profits, Being a Competitor to others in the international market, Producing unique and new products, Being a role model to others in international business.

In international business, consumer tastes vary from country to country. Traditional practices, cultures, are different. Differences in distribution channels, government interference results in variation in profit levels of a company.

Walmart, Metro cash and carry, Unilever, Ford Motor, Citi group, HP, Samsung, Sony, Dell, LG, Coca cola, Pepsi, P& G, IBM, Morgan Stanley, ING, HSBC, Metlife, Lowe's, Microsoft - Name the brand and we have it in India. Thanks to the government of INdian & their trade policies like FDI and international companies. All international players have created a lot of direct and indirect jobs in India.

38 Entrepreneurship

Entrepreneurship is for people who like to work for themselves. They create new business plans, some bring in their own capital and some borrow to start their venture. They arrange all the necessary resources. Entrepreneurship is fun, exciting, changelling, high risk, and rewarding and it's a great experience of a life time.

Entrepreneurs create lot of jobs in the market. Hence they hunt for like-minded people who like to join them and grow along with them. Some have even become millionaires after working with entrepreneurs, they create wealth for themselves and for others.

In India, millions of people have opted for entrepreneurship for their daily living and most of them have become successful.

Some of the most successful business ventures till date are : Myntra.com, Flipcart.com, Café Coffee Day, MTR Bangalore, GTR Mysore, Goli Vada Pav, Kamat Group of restaurants, Biocon. All are successful and have created lot of job opportunities in the market. Banks these days are joining hand in hand with young entrepreneurs. They are disbursing loans at nominal interest rates. But the trend has to change, banks should be more flexible and open to provide more loans to young start-ups in the country. If banks give more loans to young entrepreneurs India can achieve 100% employment & everyone will be busy at work. Everyone can either work for start-ups for some can start up on their own.

An entrepreneur usually invests his own money, sometimes even borrows money from friends, relatives, and other sources like financial institutions and bankers.

Some external financing include Angel Investors, Venture Capital Investors, most of them ask for interest, equity stake in return.

To be successful entrepreneurs you need : Vision, Mission, Dream, Aspirations, 24/7 Working Habit, Goals, Passion, Open Mind, Knowledge of Business& Industry, Tech Savvy, Knowledge of Finance, Knowledge of Market and Competition, Patience, Go Getter, Job Creator, Lovable Personality, Brand Builder, Never Say Die Attitude, Do or Die Attitude, Come what may I will do it Attitude.

There are professional institutes in India with offers training to be a entrepreneur.

So guys decide your industry, build a brand nName, create jobs for millions, millions out there are waiting for you.

39 Small and Medium Enterprises

SME is the pulse of the nation. There are many SMEs in India. Government of India has taken various steps in upbringing many SMEs. India is filled with new unique products, thanks to SMEs because some are manufactured at their places. We have the best engineering minds in the world, we can produce anything to everything in India. So we have big large scale manufacturing in larger companies. We have small & medium scale manufacturing in SMEs. As all the products cannot be manufactured at large factories, there was a need for SMEs in India. They also contribute to nation development. Young entrepreneurs took initiative to invest in SMEs. They planned what to produce, how much to produce, designed the product, created large employment opportunities for others and they sold to the world what they manufactured and created history. SMEs cater to both domestic and international markets, they create huge employments opportunities to millions in India. SMEs employs as per the standards of the industry.

So if you like to be called as a manufacturer, you like to create new trendy products, create a lot of jobs, then the answer is GO SME.

40 Advertising Management

Mudra Communications, Ogilvy, Lowe, Euro-RSCG, Hindustan Thompson, Grey, Rediffussion. are some of the best advertising agencies. They make the best ads in the country.

Advertising knowledge helps one to get into advertising world. They are both short term and full time advertising academic programs at reputed colleges. The best college according to me is the ad agency, you get hands-on experience in advertising. Advertising guys can work in PR firms, media outlets. Some can also be anchors & some talented buddies out there can even be brand managers of reputed firms and some can even start on their own.

Advertising works include : Liasioning with agency and with companies, product launches, product re-launches, creating brands, brand building efforts, photo shoots of products, making short movies. Right message and best medium of communication is very important for any advertisement, else there could be an ad clatter. Most of the top companies are busy with getting numbers that sales figures, so they all outsource their advertising and brand building works to ad agencies, they also make them responsible.

So many brands and their companies, these days everyone likes to be at the top. So everyone is on the run for brand building. The best brand recall creates more sales in the market place. Hence ad agency makes their best creative effort to be different and heard.

Various departments in ad agency are : Account Management, Creative Department, Media Department, Liasioning Works, Support Staff & Client Serving.

You could advertize in the following ways : Newspapers, magazines, print media, wall papers, radio, television, short films clips, flyers, cinema halls, transit vehicles, on buses, on trains, bill boards, hoardings, websites. All advertising works is expensive so we need to take special care of it. Message and reach is very important in advertising because our overall efforts should pay us results.

Advertising is a means where one communicates about the company, their products and services, pricing and benefits of using their products and services through visuals, videos, dance and music.

Sales promotions can be done for existing product or a new product. It is the direct method to reach consumers face to face. We include games, sampling, coupons, discounts offers.

Advertising creates more demand for goods and services in the market. It creates more production activities, it makes one buy a product or a service.

Media buying is done by advertising agency. They buy space and time and in turn sell it to companies and make profits. They buy time and space from popular newpapers and magazines and popular television and radio channels and block slots in serials, reality shows, movies, dance and music programs and then sell it to companies.

Advertising brings consumers and brands closer.

In India, celebrities like Big B, 3 Khans of Bollywood, Beautiful Ladies of Bollywood ahve sold indirectly millions of products and services.

Most popular brand recall : Thums up, Coca cola, Pepsi, Maggi, Fevicol, Lakme, Ponds, Fair & Lovely, Rasna, Tanishq, Sony, Samsung Galaxy Phones, Annapoorna atta.

41 Moral Science - Love Trees

Benefits of loving and planting more trees : You stay clam & focused. You feel pure and by watering a plant, God gives you lots of energy, You look fresh all day, You look beautiful, You will be Stress free, You get more oxygen everyday everywhere Good for the body, You will have positive attitude towards life, You will kill your demon inside, You get to see birds as they come to see plants, You will make God happy, You will have one new best friend that's love tree, You get lots of flowers, fruits, veggies from love tree, You can even earn lot of money, You will find your life filled with colors. You will get blessings, so go love tree, So many benefits, What are you waiting for love trees and plant more trees around you.

Plant more trees to get more oxygen & for a better future

42 Telecom & Mobiles

BSNL, Tata Docomo, Idea, Reliance, MTS, Airtel, Aircel - there are so many telecom players in India. They have 3G, 4G. India has a huge population, initially when these telecom players entered the market, they tied up with various mobile handsets manufacturers and started operating in India. They charged incoming and outgoing calls, call rates were higher 10 years back. Then they slowly reduced their prices, as they started getting more applications and they sold more sim cards. Later there were more telecom players in the market, incoming was free and outgoing calls were a competition. They started slowly capturing even rural India. Now telecom is like a cup of coffee, if you do not have it with you, you go missing. All telecom players have installed millions of towers across India. So you could even go roaming with your handsets. Lot of mobile handset manufacturers sold millions of products - Nokia, Samsung, Motorola, LG, Apple, Haier. Also many chinese brands entered into Indian Market. Telecom industry has created huge direct and indirect jobs in all places across India. It can be a direct job with a telecom provider or marketing handsets of various brands and even doing mobile recharge. Mobile handsets today are amazing and can do a lot of things on the go. You can watch television channels, live sports, view contents, do business, banking, internet use, movie downloads, cricket, bollywood, ringtones, mms, sms, learning, listen to music, shopping, money transfer, take a picture, send picture, share a picture or a video, face book, twitter, mobile apps & much more.

The benefits of using a mobile phone are great and fun. At the same time, one has to use it for constructive purposes, then you will enjoy more.

Today we see in India happy mobile users, all upgrade to new handsets every time a new technology is added to a phone. There is huge business and employment opportunities in this industry.

We have MBO (Multi Brand Outlets) like Sangetha, along with exclusive outlets.

Guys if you like telecom and mobiles, join this industry as it's rewarding. Jobs are available in all departments it this industry, both at exclusive stores, MBO and at telecom companies.

43 Principles of Management

MANAGEMENT is defined as human effort in making things work for a specific purpose or to achieve a certain objectives. It can be for army, hospital, school, college, company, firm or an NGO. Everyone needs good management practices for an economic growth and for overall development.

So we plan things at all levels in management, at top level, middle level, and at lower level management, all work together to achieve a certain goal in a company.

Today's market needs dynamic managers who manage things quickly & effectively, so we need to meet the company's expectation at all times. Our seniors are our mentors in our work places, we need to sit with them for hours to understand and act, so spend more time with your seniors.

Organizations means hospitals, clinics, schools, colleges, universities, companies, firms, factories. All work 24/7 for the nation.

Authority plays a very important role in management. Powers are given to people not to misuse, but in order to make the best use of it and to bring positive changes in the company, for example - SuperMan, SpiderMan, Krrish the real hero, all have authority and super powers. Result is that they protect us and their bring positive changes. Therefore whatever position you hold in the company, make the best use of your powers, please give maximum & contribute well to the company you work for. Manage things so well that it will bring great results annually.

Management is like your progress report card at schools. Now we also have a report card, an annual report card of our company. All efforts by everyone will be clearly visible in front of public, that very financial year. So be responsible for your actions every day at your offices.

Hire like-minded and interested guys who are responsible enough to bring great results, train your guys regularly, motive your employees, reward them regularly they will be more responsible for you.

In the beginning of very financial year, communicate to your employees what has to be achieved and make plans of how to achieve the same. Then every employee will be mentally prepared for their actions at work place.

Be socially responsible towards the nation, we take so much every day from the nation, so please involve company employees in some social work.

Every company has its own rules and operating principles. It varies from company to company. It can be dress-codes to behaviors at work places, ensure one thing good results and a good contributions to India.

44 Consumer Behavior

Consumer behavior is a study to find out what products and services a consumer is actually looking for, at what price, his tastes, his attitudes and his purchasing power.

Consumer has different choices today as market is filled with lots of different products and services. Customers today research through their mobile phones and tabs, compare brands and prices, then go out to the market and buy. So this is a digital world & consumers are intelligent and very particular of buying certain goods and services only.

Consumers evaluate goods and services, make a study and then buy from the market place. Celebrity influence is much higher in India. So consumers usually buy what their favorite celebrity endorses for. Celebrities make a major role in purchasing decision of a consumer. Celebrities usually enter the minds of a consumer and stay permanently, so brand recall is much higher.

Consumer behavior study helps: Companies can find out consumer likes and dislikes. Companies can find out his purchasing power. Companies can find out what motivates a consumer to buy a particular product or service. Companies can also find out various facts through questionnaires. Companies can find out what influences them to buy brands.

Practical Guess:

1. A college going girl wants to look beautiful and best all day in the college. She is now in the super market. What is she buying in the

super market?

Answer: Fair & Lovely

2. A 35 year old man is just coming out of the movie theatre, saw new Salman Khan movie - Jai Ho. He is now thirsty and wants some strong soft drink. What is he buying?

Answer: Thums Up

3. A 10 year old boy is very hungry, wants to prepare some noodles in 2 minutes. What is the boy buying from the super market? Answer: Maggi Noodles

4. A lady just now watched dove advertisement on her mobile. Now she is in the super market and looking for bathing soap for herself?

Answer: Dove

5. A family just won 2 lakh rupees from a famous reality show. They like to buy a car?

Answer: Tata Nano

This happens because of the brand recall. So brands have impact on consumer's mind.

Every company should stand in the consumer's shoes to understand, what he needs, products and services should be reachable in the hands of the end consumer. Consumer today is very cautious, intelligent, tech savvy, wants the store to look good, wants new products and services every day, wants something unique, price conscious, likes his products to be home delivered, wants credit, wants music, wants discounts, coupons. So to satisfy an Indian consumer is very challenging. So the best way is to act as a shopper and try to make your employees purchase your products. If the products are liked by your own employees, take feed back from them and then the products will automatically reach the hands of a consumer.

God has created humans, all are different, taste and interests differ, so to understand a consumer can take years, do research regularly.

45 Body Language

Body language speaks everything about a person. You can even judge a person by watching the person move.

Body language is how well we present in front of others in the society, at the market place, at interviews, at offices and even at homes. Our behaviors and actions have impact on others, so right body language is very important for everyone.

Are you happy, sad, moody, lazy, serious, workaholic? All these can be known very easily just by observing the facial and body movements of a person.

So body language is all about keeping the entire body fined tuned to different situations. In an interview we behave differently and in offices we act different. Body language is not all about customizing body moves and facial expressions. But it is a dedicated sincere approach to improve our overall personality. Body language should be good at early days at schools and slowly that becomes a habit and you remain so for the rest of your life. A student at 5th standard likes to be a doctor, his behaviors and body language was good, presentable, humble, kind, soft spoken and smiling face. He will remain like this forever, this is body language. Body language has to be practiced for many years. First have a goal in life, then your whole system will work towards it and the result is the best body language.

Body language is about carrying yourself best in all situations.

Examples of best body language, if you closely observe businessmen like Shri Ratan Tata, Shri Kumar Mangalam Birla and Shri Mukesh Ambani, all carry themselves well all day in all situations. They are the face of country's biggest enterprises, so their body language is the best at all times. Body language is an art which has to be practiced for many years.

So have the best body language because someone out there is watching us closely.

46 Organization Behavior

ORGANIZATION behavior helps one to find out how employees and various departments behave in a given organization after a careful detailed study inside the organization. Human Resource departments can bring various measures to make its organization effective. Employees are the biggest assets in any organization, hence we need to ensure that employees function well at their jobs. Any problems at organization level should not affect their minds.

Organization behavior is like a 360 degree check on employees, groups, team leaders, department heads and its overall organization. By doing this activity we can perform better and if necessary, we can bring necessary changes in the work place.

There are many theories in organization behavior. OB also checks how an employee behaves inside the work place and outside the work place. Deep understanding of an employee is good for any organization. Some can bring positive changes in the organization and some can also bring negative changes in the organization, by their behaviors and actions.

Organization study helps organization : We can check our employee behaviors. We can check what motivates them to work better, improves attendance among employees, reduces attrition. We can check whether an employee is suitable for a given job. We can bring many changes in the organization after counseling with employees. We can do job rotation for some employees. We can promote some good employees in the organization. We can give additional responsibilities to those who have less work at organization. We can find ways to build better relationship with employees. We can stay ahead of competetion as there is good support from employees. Fights and harassments can be identified at work places. Fear factor among employees of losing a job now will not be there. We can provide new training activities for employees. Organization profits grow faster, more production at factory. All employees will be happy after a new change in the organization, they will be charged to work, will spend more time in the organization, will earn more incentives. New changes can be a new building, new interiors, cafeteria, new benefits, more incentives leading to employees staying happy and loyal to the organization.

47 Strategic Management

STRATEGIC Management is like a chess game, we have all the resources, capital, manpower, good products and services in front of us. We have opponents who block our way, our competitors, so we need to make the best move. In today's competitive market and entry of foreign players, consumers are getting more choosy. Most of the businesses are lost because of margins and other factors, so a given company has to formulate and implement the best possible plans in order to be alive in the market.

Strategic management study help us : It helps us to make plans. It helps one to formulate moves, to implement the best course of action in the market. It helps to scan both internal and external environments, helps us to achieve both short-term and long-term objectives of the company. It gives a new direction for our organization. It will act like a facilitator and a guide and a mentor, helps in building and achieving new targets for our products and services, helps us to find new potential customers, helps in entering new markets, i.e. we can now reach the untapped markets, thereby increases our sales. We can achieve higher sales and more profits. We can also identify new training requirements for our employees to achieve better results, helps in upgrading to new technology and processes so that we stay ahead in business, creates new opportunities, we can venture into new businesses. Strategic management principles followed properly can give a new powerful company, help a company to contribute higher to a nation's economic growth, helps us to produce new products, creates more jobs. Our employees stay happy leads to new happy company.

In order to stay active in the market, we should see our competition, substitute products and services and negotiators.

Minimum inputs, maximum outputs, one hit, two competitors, out of the market, should be the strategy. One should make strong moves so that competitors fear and run from the market.

Strategy formulation is not enough, we need to implement our strategy and we should ensure it works. So strategy is a planned move in business.

In order to have better moves, we need SWOT, Strength, Weakness, Opportunity and Threat.

Example: Café Coffee Day

Strength: Brand name, more outlets, long presence in the market, better service, latest food menus, own coffee plantations, latest technology, more division like coffee vending machines, espresso outlets and coffee powder selling outlets.

Weakness: Targeted for youth, not reachable for all customers. There price for a cup of a regular coffee comes close to Rs 50 and if someone likes to buy snacks, it's expensive. So not all customers visit Café Coffee Day.

Opportunity: Can build more outlets, can sell the brand and can make a lot of money and can utilize the space with other marketing guys, in turn can generate more profits.

Threats: New young entrepreneurs are coming with new concept, Coffee and Chai stores so slowly business in future will be taken over by young entrepreneurs.

So guys play your best moves.

48 Human Relations Skills

In society, a human should love a human, human should interact with many humans. It is good for us because there will be lots of knowledge transfer and you will understand their needs and wants. Humans should help one another, humans should be united, multiply all humans if all work, for a cause and all have a common goal in the company. Then your company is on the Moon and you could even build a new nation which will be the most powerful on this planet.

In companies, we meet humans with different cultural backgrounds, traditional values, dress styles. Everyone will have huge expectations from the company so we need to be always helpful to each other in the company.

We need to build a healthy and good relationship with one another to perform better in the organization. This is human relations. God has given us plenty of water, food, clothing, shelter, mobile, internet, cash, gold, silver, good parents, loved ones, friends for support, entertainment. So many things so be happy for what you have and try to make others happy and most important make your company happy and give best results.

In any company, HR managers are like God fathers, he or she should direct everyone on right paths, so that everyone stays happy and is successful and brings great results to the company.

Basic Human Relations Skills :Love all humans, birds, animals, love tree. Respect everyone, employees, suppliers, distributors, franchisee owners, CEO, MD, Managers, Directors, Sub-ordinates, workers, housekeeping staffs, security. Treat everyone as equals, listen to people's concerns at your work place. Bring in a fun-based atmosphere, be co-operative with your team members, do not misguide any one, do not give wrong facts and figures, be ethical in your approach, do not encourage or do negative things which harm company's reputation, be cool, be Nice, be colorful, be soft spoken, work smart, do not get into fight at work places, respect women at work places, build good rapport among all departments in the company, be a leader and direct everyone on right paths, be a role model to society, bring in positive changes in the company which you work for, give suitable suggestions and improve processes so that organization makes more profits, give your 100%.

Love and care is the answer for better human relations at work places.

49 Employee Counseling

EMPLOYEE Counseling is one of the most important and a must for all the organizations. It can be for small, medium and large enterprises. A human resource manager should make a point that he or she should counsel all their employees at least once in three months to achieve greater heights in business. In today's fast business environments, our employees will be psychologically in pain, in ill-health, stressed, lose focus in their jobs, lack concentration, be angry, lose their cool regularly, no respect to any one, care free, family problems in mind, no goals, no charge, no motivation towards work, monetary oriented and not work oriented. Employee counseling is a great vital tool to solve employees' short and long term psychological problems. What is there in their minds can be easily found after a detailed counseling with all employees. So it's a great benefit for both employee and employer in a organization. If your employees are sick, counseling is a must to make them healthy and wealthy. When employee is ill, his overall productivity comes down and profits dips. We can even bring in a counselor on board to conduct their employee counseling. There are many experts in the industry today, they will do this work for us.

A counselor will usually sit face to face with the employees and understand the problems and will also solve the problems.

Some major benefits of employee counseling to the organization : Helps to identify and solve employees problems. All employees will be in good health, productivity will be higher, happy employees and happy company. All employees are now charged and can also now take new and higher responsibilities and achieve the tasks. An employee get promotions and employers make more profits, mutually benefitted scenario, cool, new, high energy, fully charged company and its employees. Employees stay loyal to their organizations and try to work for more years in the same organization leading to more profits in balance sheets. A company which is engaged in employee counseling will also be a bench mark for others in the market, others will also follow and it will be good for the nation.

50 Supply Chain & Distribution Management

Supply Chain management is the management of movement of goods - raw material goods to factory inventory points, then from finished goods to distributor points, then from distributor points to end consumer homes.

So supply chain is inter-connected and this requires careful planning, execution, monitoring and control.

Distribution Management on the other hand is also movement of goods from raw material supplier point to factory point or manufacturer point to sale point. The activities include inventory, supply chain, ware housing, stockings, logistics, packaging.

For any company, movement of goods is very important. It can be for small, medium and large companies.

Time, cost, energy, manpower goes into moving the goods from one place to another so we have to ensure that we effectively manage our distribution works.

Example : A company is into production of ready to use masala powders. It has a small factory and has appointed 16 distributors across Bangalore city. It's product range include rasam powder, sambar powder, egg masala powder, chicken masala powder, kabab masala and it produces 1000 kgs of mix masala powders per day.

Plan of Action from factory head :

1. He will have meetings with his 16 distributors. A distributor has to pick ready masala from factory and then he has to stock at their godowns and then he has to supply to retailers, hyper markets, wholesalers. By doing this, he is saving cost and ensuring that new production packs reach the end consumer fast.

2. He will also have meetings with production teams and ensure 1000 kgs of mix masala is ready every day, production chart is also ready at the place for action.

3. He will have meetings with raw material suppliers and ensure that raw material reaches on time.

By doing a perfect supply chain, the company is now producing and marketing 3,65,000 kgs per year. Right Management of Goods = More profits = Happy Customers& Happy Company.

Someone out there is waiting for you, to buy your products, so have the best supply chain in place.

51 B2B

B2B is meant to facilitate transactions between a raw material supplier and manufacturer and so on. B2B builds better and strong relationships between a supplier and buyers. B2B is most vital and most important for any company. B2B is not one time buying and selling, it happens repeatedly, round the clock and round the year. So for all these transactions to make it happen, one has to keep a good relationship among one another. B2B helps in nation's prosperity. B2B saves time, cost, energy and movement of goods is easy. B2B also creates new business opportunities and also creates jobs.

Examples:

1. A manufacturer from automobile industry makes cars. In order to make cars,he needs thousands of parts which goes into car making. If you open your car, you could find thousands of parts in it. Car manufacturer is not in the business of making parts but is in the business of making cars. So how does he assemble and sell so may units? Answer is B2B = Outsourced. He will outsource all the parts, he will make others manufacture to supply parts for him. All major parts are outsourced like leather, tyres, nuts, bolts, rubber, steel, iron, windshields, audio & video systems, seats, sunroof, wipers, glass, mounted steering wheels, maag wheels, bumpers, stickers, chrome, air conditioning, anti braking systems, alarms. air bags, horns, remote locking. If B2B does not happen,

you will not find new cars moving in the market. So B2B is very important.

2. A soft drink manufacturer need syrup, sugar, water, bottles, preforms, to make a soft drink. A soft drink manufacturer does not make bottles, but he will outsource, that's B2B. All suppliers will supply all these items at the right time and help a soft drink maker to produce more soft drinks, so B2B helps one to be mutually benefitted.

Hence B2B is very important for any business. We need to ensure that we keep our suppliers happy all the time. And most important is negotiation, good deal makes more profits and bad deal can make you lose and out of the market, so one has to hire a good negotiator or a purchase manager who has good raw material knowledge and also is good at negotiations with vendors. This brings good business opportunities plus more profits.

B2C on the other hand, is selling goods directly to consumers. Some manufacturers are engaged in the business of selling goods directly to end consumers, like teleshopping, online sales and direct marketing channels and even multi level marketing methods. By doing this, a manufacturer makes more profits plus he will not share his profits with others in the market.

B2G is that manufacturers will be engaged in supplying their products to government departments through tenders or through direct orders like BHEL, BEML.

52 International Marketing

Are you happy selling your products locally? Do you like to enter into new markets and international markets? So one needs gyaan of international marketing. Marketing is the same, even same in international marketing. But one has to follow rules & regulations set by the other country. We need to obey them strictly at any cost. As one country is allowing us to international markets, we should respect that and take great care in following them.

International marketing: You can export your goods into another country. Country which is rich in natural resources can export their surplus raw materials goods to the country who is in need of it. International marketing also helps one to know each other well, i.e. one manufacturer in India will be able to make a connection with another buyer in UK. By selling goods and services to another country in one way we also are helping another country. Example - India is rich in coffee, tea, spices and other goods, we can export the same to the international markets. China is known for making unique and mass production of their goods. Hence we can import certain goods which are in demand in Indian market. You can enter into international markets by franchising & joint ventures by signing different contracts and agreements. You could also make customized goods which suit international markets, for example, Gokuldas, a garment manufacturer in India produce garments as per their orders from international markets. Their sizes, styles, stitching patterns, prints, embroidery vary from order to order and are different from country to country. International Marketing creates lot of business and jobs opportunities both locally and in the international markets. You could even do online marketing by selling a complete range of products to reach the global customer like amazon.com. International Marketing makes a firm popular and heard, more profits as you are an international company. You get profits from all countries, for example - Arvind Mills is the world's biggest manufacturer of denims, it produces and sells denim materials to almost all the major brands worldwide. They are producing Flying Machine jeans locally and making profits and also selling denim materials to biggest brands like Wrangler, Tommy, etc. worldwide and making profits even in the international markets. Arvind Denim materials is world famous because the finish and the quality is at its best all the time. Your brand will be in the minds of a global customer for example - KFC, McDonald's, Tommy Hilfiger, Armani, CAT, USPA, Coca Cola, Pepsi. Indian fashion designers are also popular in international markets by showcasing their unique garments in the international markets. Pepsi, Coca Cola & Unilever are the classy examples of how they operate worldwide. They have made their brands a household name. There is an opportunity to make your company listed in International stock exchanges. Company is happy as they have international presence, customers are happy because they can now experience international products. Suppliers of raw materials & investors, stakeholders all are happy as company is doing well. You could make our country proud by entering international markets. Hence, know your products, know your strengths and opportunities in front of you. Make a perfect marketing plan, have meetings with consultants and your staff members, take suitable guidance, follow rules and code of conduct and make more profits in international markets.

53 Yoga

YOGA is a continuous learning. One has to be in perfect condition to face our daily busy life. Hence we need to learn and practice yoga, we can practice yoga either at home, offices or even you could enrol for professional yoga classes. Yoga is an ancient practice by gurus. Yoga makes you look cool, smart, intelligent, talented, focused, energetic, flexible, social and a contributor.

Some benefits of yoga: You get peace of mind, you care for others and yourself - a well being. You feel relaxed, it improves blood circulation, respiratory functions and you have a good digestive system. It gives you lot of energy. You start loving yourself, others on this planet - birds, animals, trees and all living creatures on this planet. You bring in some positive changes in the work place and in the society. You will start contributing in your own way to your country. Personal career grows, helps you to focus. It fine tunes your body and mind, you get ill rarely. You gain knowledge, intelligence quotient and emotional quotient improves and you start getting better grades in your exams. Nervous system will be at its best. You stay happy, stay fresh all day. Some people who are fat can now lose their weight. Immunity increases, you breathe easy. You will respect yourself, parents and others on this planet. No need of protein shakes, you will get a makeover. You will maintain good relation with others. Others start liking you, you get good quality sleep. You will get a perfect body balance. You will get inner satisfaction. You will be useful to others. So many benefits and the list goes on and on. So guys, if you are working or a student, yoga is fun and makes you rock and look cool, so go yoga.

54 Brand Management

Any brand is like a family member to a company. Take care of them like babies, watch them grow, love your own brands. So a brand needs management, Brand Management helps one to know your product, know your target market, know your competitors and helps you to research and market your brand much better. We need good planning, analysis, feed back, dedicated sales force, right advertising mantras which goes well and most important is to be in the mind of the consumer. If a brand does well, you make lot of profits. So if your brand has to do well in the market, you need right connection with the consumer. Brand does well, you produce right product and make them reach at the right time in the hands of the consumer, if you do this you gain competitive advantage.

Some common household brands : Milk - KMF - Nandini, Coffee - Bru, Nescafe, Cothas, Tea - Tata Tea, Taaza, Coffee Hang Out - Café Coffee Day, Tooth Paste - Colgate, Fairness Cream - Fair & Lovely, Ready to Eat Snacks - MTR, Haldirams, Soap - Dove, Cinthol, Lifeboy, Lux, Mysore Sandal, Shampoo - All Clear, Noodles - Maggi, Masala powder - MTR, Rice Cooker - Prestige, Fridge - Samsung, Washing Machine - Whirlpool, Mobile Handset - Samsung, Nokia, Telecom Service Provider - Tata Docomo, Idea Cellular, Cars - Honda City, BMW, Tata Nano, Jeeps - Maruthi Gypsy, Mahindra, Super Market - More, Nilgiris, Food world, Hyper Market - Metro Cash and Carry, Big Bazaar, More, Ice Cream -

Kwality Walls, Chocolates - Dairy Milk, Biscuits - Parle G, Television - Sony, Music System - Bose, Management Education - IIM Bangalore.

So many brands these days, only few reaches homes. It is quite a big and challenging task for an company. Brand building does not happen in one day. It takes years of hard work from millions of employees, advertising agencies, brand managers efforts, good and bright appealing products, and much more. So companies have to produce a right product to their target consumers. Then brands get popular, company is happy and consumer is also happy.

A Brand Manager plays a very important role. Some skills required are : He should have a management qualification with technical expertise, good communication skills, should take responsibility of a brand or a group of brands, should be passionate, should be well organized in his activities, good presentation skills, should develop right ads, market research & sales promotions, should have regular meeting with his sales team, should have a habit of working 24/7 for his brand. He should love his brand & also make others to love the brand, should create right market for his brand, reach - should make the brand available in the market at the right time, should make competitive moves in the market, should make the brand live longer and should be dedicated.

So guys isn't it interesting? Love brands and manage brands. Big brands like Fair & Lovely, Lux, Thums up are much larger than any big company so their brand value is high. One has to take special care & love your brands, if you love your brands the rest will be history.

55 Marketing Research

MARKETING research is a study of knowing facts and figures from the market place and from the consumer. It involves knowing what's there in the consumer's mind and what are their expectations from a products or a service. One can get to know even how a particular product or a service behaves in the market place.

Marketing Research helps a firm : Helps one to collect data from the market place and also from the consumers. It is an organized study where one gets to know a consumer, a competitor, a market, target market, pricing, new business opportunities, positioning a product or a service, consumer experiences. It helps one to gather and record data for future use of the firm, helps a firm to gain competitive advantage in the market, helps a firm to replace a product if it is outdated in the market, for example new technology changes the way we live. So technology product manufacturers research both in the market place and with the consumers to know what best new tech products can be introduced. It helps a firm to do right pricing for their products and services, helps a firm to connect directly with the consumer through questionnaires and direct interviews with the consumers, helps a firm to know the past, present and future trends about their industry, brands, products, services, competitors, helps a firm to produce right goods and services, as per the demands of the market place and consumers. A firm and its employees will be knowledge and they can prepare themselves for future actions. **Market Research is of two types -**

Primary data collection - data which will be collected from the market place and consumers for future use and actions,

Secondary data - readily available data like annual reports and magazines, and blogs.

Hence, MR brings a lot of benefits to the organization, so we need to make the best use of gathered data and make perfect action plans, so that we gain competitive advantage and make more profits.

All new products and services which we see today in the market place is the result of the marketing research. Marketing research helps one to see new products and services in the future.

Example - Off Road, On Road Bike - Hero Impulse - We never had a bike of this format after MR, Hero made Impulse Motor Bike for office goers and for college buddies & also for action heroes.

56 International Human Resource Management

HRM is the overall management of manpower in an organization, finding a right person, from screening to short listing, organizing interviews, hiring the best man who suits the organization requirements, induction, training and development, counseling, performance appraisal, promotions, transfers, compensation management, well-being, making him work with us longer.

When the firm goes global, we need more manpower for our daily operational requirements, sometimes we send our home country staff on foreign assignments and sometimes we hire from the place we do business, that is locals. So all the human resource activities at international level is known as IHRM. Activities are more or less the same of HRM except a few activities like expatriate management, training and development, suitable compensation which matches international standards.

IHRM manages manpower in all the countries where it operates. Sometimes we may have to shuffle our employees, due to work demands. Some employees are good at some things, so we need to shuffle as and when required.

Some benefits of IHRM :You get the best talented people to work for you locally and globally. An organization will be very strong now as they have the best manpower with them. They all can be united and sky is the limit now to achieve our goals. They work together and solve problems, they invent, bring in new collective ideas to improve things at organization level. An MNC looks rich, colorful, powerful both inside and outside. A Indian company which is doing well will also do well in the rest of the world, example is TCS, Infosys, Wipro. Knowledge transfer happens quickly and the organization now looks like a big library. Both employees and employer are very happy. Customer worldwide is happy. With international presence, more & new products can be introduced by the firm. Organization gets bigger and bigger as more profits come in globally.

The most important work in IHRM is managing foreign manpower. We need to take care of them well and we need to give them best compensation packages as per the standards, safety and security at work and take care of their health and their family members, accommodation facilities, training, promotion, new roles assignments, extra perks and incentives. HR department has to fulfill all their needs and aspirations, and most important is the human touch factor.

57 Labor Laws

Labor laws are made for the welfare and protection of the workers. So every organization has to learn and follow all the rules and regulations which are made by the government. For workers' protection, you can terminate any employee if and only if he misbehaves or is absent or causes direct or indirect damages to the organization. There is All India Organization for employees, there will be labor officer appointed by the government, who visits your organization and ensures that you follow rules and take care of employees well. There will be surprise visits from a labor officer to a factory so one has to be very careful. Workers can even approach labor departments of state to solve their issues. Trade unions also protect the workers at factory level. So ever HR manager should know all the principles and rules and operate accordingly.

Some acts : ESI, EPF, Factories Act, The Workmen Compensation Act, Weekly Holidays, Minimum Wage Act, Bonus Act, Standard working hours with breaks, The Contract labor act. A worker works day and night and makes his owner's dream come true. So we need to keep them happy all the time, and provide them all the necessary things during and after the work. So never forget a worker, all businesses are standing in the market only because of our workers. So we need to treat them with respect and care for them all the time. If you go to big factories, like Titan, all employees are taken care so well, factory premises is clean, neat, hygienic, good working environment, good staff members, food facility - good nutritional meal is served for their workers, transport, housing, and many facilities are provided by the Tata group. Tata group is a classy example of how they take care of their workers, and they also follow rules of the government, with no complaint from workers, Hence its is one of the highly respected Business House in the Country.

In foreign countries, they have their own laws to protect their workers. So let make our workers happy and let stand united to build a new India.

58 Corporate Gifting

CORPORATE gifting is a business of supplying unique customized gifts to corporate. It's a great business to be in, because you can make a lot of money, and you make corporate and their employees also happy. Different corporate gifting companies customize gifts as per their client requirements, there are many corporate gifting firms operating in India. It's a highly profitable business to be in, the various gifts supplied are chocolates, goodie hampers, wall clocks, pens, t-shirts with embroidery and customized prints, pen drives, mobile phones, key chains, desktop items, wooden items, glass ware, gift coupons, caps, jackets, trousers, shirts, cricket team t-shirts, laptops, laptop bags, bag packs, jute bags, smiley balls, trophies, wrist watches, gold and silver coins. and much more. Corporate gifts are customized as per the client requirements and it varies from order to order. Usually a corporate gifting firm will have tie up with all the vendors, after getting the order they work with them and supply the same to various corporate. One could start this business with small capital and after they start getting more orders they can rise and be big in the industry. This industry has created a millions of indirect jobs in major metros in India. One needs goods contacts in industry to start gifting business. I have seen employees being happy after their get gifts from their employers or companies.

Happy Gifting

59 Compensation Management

COMPENSATION management is all about giving right compensation for the work done by our employees, as per the designations we need to match industry standards all the time. Every one works for money, so we need to pay our employees well so that they work hard and stay longer with us. Compensation should cover basics like Basic Salary, House Rent Allowance, Travelling Allowance, Special Allowance, Provident Fund, Medical Benefits, Travel Insurance, Accident Insurance, Child Education, Incentives based on quarterly performance of employees and so on. Compensation packages vary from department to department and from designation to designation. But we need to follow certain standards in today's business, because today we see rentals have gone up in all major cities in India. Cost of monthly maintenance, children education is expensive, we need to look at employees' basic needs before designing a compensation package. Today most of the MNCs operating in India are paying their employees well with all the facilities, things have changed in some sectors and some sectors still need improvements.

Benefits of Good Compensation Package : Employees will be happy, employees' family members will be happy, builds trust, motivates employees, employees stay loyal, they work hard and contribute maximum to their companies, they bring faster results, more sales, more happiness, profits go up.

60 Performance Management

Do you want to make your organization look powerful, then you need performance management. Performance management helps one to improve performance of their employees. This is a complete transformation activity, every company has to perform well in today's competitive market. The same applies to even our employees. Employees should perform like superstars everyday so that they bring in positive changes. It should be a win-win situation for both sides. Performance is good for overall organization because, if all stay united and perform well then bring good results on board, then it's a happy company. So we need to ensure all employees perform well in all the departments in the company, because if their performance parameter dips then all go upside down, and we even incur loses. So in order to improve the organization's performance, we need to check our present status, future business plans and actions, company's quarterly and annual targets, departments wise scanning, allocating work, training activities, employees health is important if an organization has to perform. You need to perform well everyday well because someone out there will take advantage if we do not perform, that's Performance Management.

61 Modern Manager

Modern Manager is cool, dynamic, powerful, smart, intelligent, tech savvy, management graduate, multi-skilled person, sports enthusiast, likes music & dance, entertainer, contributor, rocker, go getter, winner, can take big challenges, workaholic, knowledgeable, industry expert, experienced, good looking, organizer, mentor, fitness freak, likes horse riding and rock climbing, likes to be a billionaire, he works like a entrepreneur, he is like a king. So managers are the face of any company. A modern manger brings more happiness, fun and excitement at work, more trust, more sales, more positive changes, he works like a SuperMan in a company. So any company who is hiring mangers should hire the best because they bring in complete change, implement new ideas, new sales orders, more wealth, and more happiness. So hire mangers who are like kings who are ready to hit the market from day one.

62 Sales Management

SALES Management is all about managing sales departments and their managers, sales teams, hiring right sales force, induction and training, compensation packages, incentive slabs, product launches, and order management, market feed backs, observing competition, allocation territories to staff, dealer management.

Sales department is one of the most important departments in any company. So we need to manage this well because money comes in to the business from sales orders.

Practical Example : New construction company is constructing new apartments in Electronic City Bangalore. The company has kept a target of 100 Crores for this project, It has 1 sales head, 5 institutional sales managers, and 5 indoor sales managers and sales representatives. Now we need to break our sales targets and fix targets for sales managers and their teams. Then we need to train our sales staff, then we need to assign them areas, then we need to monitor them, have regular sales meetings, most important is motivate your sales team that if they do early bookings then there is lot of incentives waiting for them.

Most important in sales is you need to get business. If one gets business, he earns or else there is no mutual benefit, so hire super sales guys who likes sales and who likes to make a lot of money.

Sales guys today take away big fat cheques as incentives every month. Making everyone taking incentive cheques is the true meaning of Sales management, because they all have orders in hand, company is happy & sales guys are also happy.

Happy Selling

63 Event Management

Event Management is making client events successful. It can be a new product launch, wedding, exhibitions, prelaunch, distributing flyers, road shows, press meet and conferences, movie launch, corporate anniversary, birthday parties, corporate annual parties, silver jubilee& golden jubilee celebrations at corporate, festival celebrations, marketing research campaigns, concerts, events, fashion shows, college day celebrations, from a smallest fair to a big corporate celebration, event management show ensure that it manages all the activities well and make the event very successful.

Event manager plays a very important role in making every event very successful. He visits the client place to discuss about the event, take details of the type of event, design a suitable plan and budget for the event, gets the deal to organize the event, then he start making budget planning, manpower planning, communication strategy, his creative art works, event designing, organize meeting with different vendors like music, lights, production, logistics. He will do the site visits, client servicing, cash flow management, scheduling the event, testing, will also take precautions for health and safety like drinking water, first aid, and fire safety equipments. He organizes lights, video, play sound, talk with artist, etc. Event management works vary depending on the nature of event, but making it successful is the main task of event manager.

If you have seen the Bollywood movie Band Baaja Baraat, you could see how a marriage event management company organizes various marriages. Actor and Actress in the movie customize wedding functions as per their client budgets and requirements.

There are some professional institutes which award you certificate in event management and you could even work in hospitality, travel, advertising agencies, hotels, corporate, NGO, media.

Opportunities are huge in India if one likes to get into event management. You could even start your own business in event management, get deals, organize and plan events and make them successful. You get more clients on board and you can be an established player in the market offering only event management solutions for all types of events.

Today if you see most of the awards functions, model shows, exhibitions, big weddings, ceremonies, birthday and concerts, movie launches all are managed by big event management groups in the country.

Some event management companies are bigger than any company today because they host a lot of events worldwide and make them successful.

64 Rural Marketing

MAJORITY of the Indian population still lives in rural India. Rural India is filled with opportunities for new young entrepreneurs. Literacy rate is improved from the past ten years and is going up every year. Hence rural population has awareness of brands, products and services. Rural India agriculture contribution is immense. Most of the brands have already reached Indian rural markets and are doing very well, example - Coca Cola, Pepsi, thums up, UB Beer, Kingfisher, Smirnoff Vodka, Tide, Wheel, Wills Cigarette, Tata tea, Tata Coffee, Tata Salt, Godrej Soaps, Parle G, Britannia Biscuits, Maggi Noodles, Ready to Eat - MTR, Halidirams, Renault Duster, Maruthi Gypsy, Mahindra Tractors, Tata Buses, Ashok Leyland Trucks, Hero Honda, Nokia, Samsung, LG, Refrigerator, Washing Machines, LCD TVs, Maruthi 800, Lux, Colgate, MTS mobiles, Airtel, BSNL, laptops, music systems, name the brand and it's now available in the rural market.

Some rural Indians are now constructing some beautiful landmark homes for themselves, so they use the best technologies even in the rural market. Rural India is extremely doing well and is contributing to India's growth and development.

HUL has made significant investments in the rural markets. They launched their products and also made them work, that is the power of Rural India. They also improve the life style of millions of rural Indians. Hero Honda has dealers spread across India. Many automobile giants have been benefitted after tapping the rural market. Government of India has also made large investments in training rural Indians to achieve new skills like tailoring, embroidery, printing, computer education, baking, cooking, painting, selling skills, farming, call center training, candle making, data entry, English speaking, etc.

Many NGOs has helped people to get the best education, housing, nutrition, healthcare.

So guys rural India has Colgate, Lux, All Clear, TATA Tea, Magg, Sony LCD TV, TATA Sky, Samsung Galaxy Mobile phone, Samsung Laptops, Whirlpool Washing machine, Prestige Cookers, LIC. Our country has also produced best actors, musicians, theatre personalities, framers, super rich people, best doctors, best engineers, best clothing, best food, best water, best homes. Rural India is rich, colorful, vibrant and powerful, so guys make the best use of this amazing opportunity - our rural India.

Hence, you should market your products and services so that they recall. If rural India can recall your brands the rest is history. One has to do sampling, do exhibition, melas, call people & showcase your products and I am sure if they like it then it gets viral in rural India.

Many movies and many brands have done extremely well in rural India so tap the rural India.

65 Economics

Economics helps : To find how market, industry & population behaves in a country. It helps to research the minds of a customer, helps to find the needs and wants of a family, group, and individuals in a city or a group of cities. It gives us accurate results after the study. It helps one to get facts and figures of population, industry, business units, SMEs, firms, partnership firms, private limited companies, public limited companies, products, services, brands, facilities, infrastructures, current financial position of country, future growth prospects, trade and commerce, currency, exchange rates, banking, stock exchange, taxes. Economics is of great use for all, helps to frame policies and procedures, it uses the knowledge of math's, science, social, commerce, and business studies. It helps to solve both long term and short term problems of any situation in business. This study is a great use for the nation. There are many economists who are constantly researching on various topics. It helps us to view situations at a micro and at a macro level. It studies human behavior, the impact on political influences, the scarcities of resources of a region or of a whole country. It helps the marketing departments to do right sales promotional activities in the market. It helps one to introduce right product and services in the market. It helps one to choose right manufacturing locations, right products to produce, how much to produce and it helps a firm to achieve economies of scale. It helps one to know the sources of financing for business. It builds new markets, export & import trade opportunities, nations, educate people.

It creates new demands in the market for a product or a service and it also helps to do demand forecasting of a particular brand, product or service. By this a firm can efficiently operate in the market. It helps a firm to know its target audience. One can be knowledgeable after the economics study knowledge transfer. It makes a country powerful, knowledgeable, rich, prosperous and a happy country.

So guys there are great benefits of studying economics. It is very essential to have a knowledge of economics so one has to do research more about economics because it is beneficial for us to contribute to our India.

66 Being Artistic - Sketch-Draw-Paint-Craft

ART is fun and is very important for the overall development of employees. It is a great benefit for the entire organization - so Draw - Paint - Sketch - Or Do Craft Work at work, home or when you get free time.

Art helps : You love people around you. It makes you learn more and more, you start loving all subjects and thereby you improve your knowledge. It makes you quick, makes you think and adapt. It improves your creativity at work, you reduce your mistakes at work, brain will be active 24/7. It helps you to solve problems, it helps one to give new ideas and suggestions at work, you make others happy and comfortable at work. You become open-minded, you stay focused in work, you will be a sharp thinker. It controls your emotions and you start expressing your feelings. You lose fear and anxiety at work, you stay enthusiastic. What is on your mind is on the paper now. It improve health conditions, you enter a new world of happiness. All your goals and targets at work place will be met. Your dreams will be true, you stay healthy, calm & relaxed. You bring in great results for your organization. It is fun time every day, you be a go getter. You will bring in a new environment at work and Happy Company = Happy Employees.

So many benefits for both employees and employers, hence human resource managers should organize painting, drawing, sketching, craft work at work place frequently so that it will be benefitted to the organization and its employees and the result is a happy company and happy employees.

67 Moral Science - Social Service

HUMAN beings should love and respect each other, irrespective of our caste system. Due to karmas some are born rich and poor, but for God all are equals and same. God has given plenty of water, food, clothing, shelter, resources on this planet. He is seeing how we make best use of these resources and live happy. But due to greed we will not enjoy the resources which are created by God. Hence God and all religious books and regions say one thing in common, that is
"Make your body, soul, mind, cash, resources, land, water, builidngs, property, knowledge, education, skills useful for others on this Planet."

So, you should not only work for yourself, parents, relatives and friends, but you should also make the best use of your resources for others. Every rupee you earn comes from the public, so give back to society in any form every day.
"Someone is waiting for you - So please go help"

Today you could see many NGOs working on various causes for : health, poor & needy, for aged - help age foundation, child - child rights, children education, sick, orphanages, skill development, social security, housing, food, clothing, handicaped, sanitation, better bathrooms, public tiolets, love birds, love animals, love dogs, love street dogs, love trees. All are doing their best to help others and to make this planet a better place to live in.

All these NGOs are made by God for the benefit of humans, birds, animals, trees and all living creatures on this planet. He likes us to be happy - the God.

Charity should be started in your young age, parents should help their children learn how to help. You should teach them how to share food, clothing, shelter, and other resources with others who are in need. Parents and teachers are the right people to make them learn about helping others - help a needy everyday makes one's life beautiful and worth a living.

Even after so many NGOs in the market, I can see : poor children & aged who like to have good food - no money. Poor children wish to educate themselves - no proper access to education, poor children & aged need shelter - no facilities to stay. Slums are reduced across the country but even today you can see few of them. Beggars are in plenty, begging in streets, traffic signals, temples, roads and other places for food, clothing and shelter. I can see rich people becoming richer every day and poor remain poor in India. I can see people wasting lot of money in malls, high streets, shopping, festivals, celebrations, movies or jewellery. All for our temporary satisfaction, greater satisfaction is always in helping others on this planet.

So guys wake up, they are lots of people waiting for you and me on this planet. Be and take responsibility for one, ten, hundred, thousand or even more. Ms Nita Ambani - Reliance recently took 18,000 under privileged children to watch an IPL match 2014. So even some big and famous celebrities are taking responsibility towards others. By helping others you gain more strength and God gives you more to help more people. So do your bit and make India proud.

"To help you need not be rich, all you need is - I need to help others mantra - If you have this in you - God gives you the rest"

68 Playing with Numbers & Data - Business Maths & Statistics

Numbers 0,1,2,3,4,5,6,7,8,9 will be with us all our life. It remained with us in schools and colleges and we use numbers in our day to day life, and it helps us in all our business transactions. We need to know how to play with numbers, it's fun and also interesting, we have percentages, calculations, addition, subtraction, division, multiplication, averages, simple algebra, calculating simple and compound interest rates, sets, etc. All these gyaan will be used to record and use it for our future needs. If one has to be successful in business, maths is very essential. Business maths can be used for marketing, sales forecasting, banking, where to invest, how much to invest, manufacturing, trading, demand forecasting, helps to achieve economies of scale, and to solve real life business problems. Business maths is for all who like to make a lot of money. It is important for business houses, individuals, business owners, managers, real estate people for their calculations on commission rates, mortgages, taxes, for wealth mangers to multiply money, for tax consultants, for buying and selling goods and services. So love maths and love numbers and start playing with numbers to be successful in business.

Statistics on the other hand, use data and numbers. It analyses, interprets data to give businesses a complete report for future use, in the form of charts, diagrams, pie charts, analysis reports, and complete report on the research.

Statistics helps us in : decision making, solving business problems, sales forecasting, observe Competition's moves, to introduce suitable products and services in the market, know the population, needs and wants of a consumer, policy making, monitoring, to get best deals, negotiation, controlling, benefits are many.

So learn business maths and statistics for all your day to day needs.

69 Business Law

SECURITIES law, intellectual property law, labor law, employment law, immigration law, income tax, commercial paper, bankruptcy, Indian corporate law, secured transactions, essential commodities act, company law, partnership law, sale of goods and services, foreign exchange management act, foreign exchange regulation act, Indian contract act, Arbitrations, all laws are to protect the owner and business enterprises.

All laws are made in business so that you play in the boundaries set by the government & then if one breaks the rules one has to pay a price - Business Law. It protects one and by these laws one can do business smoothly and effectively.

Under Companies act, Indian employees are protected, there are payment of wages act, industrial employment act, industrial disputes act, payment of bonus act, payment of gratuity act. There is also copyrights act to protect music makers in India. It checks and protects from frauds. Business law is of great use in our daily business transactions, one cannot get away easily by committing a fraud in the market place, you and I are protected by these business laws.

Business laws helps one : to do business smoothly, to do business effectively, to obey laws and to be good citizens, protects from fraud, controlling and monitoring, bring more profits, more employment opportunities in the markets, start new businesses, creates new business opportunities, one could do more business, companies can introduce new products and services.

Business laws are for all those who are engaged in business, laws are made to benefit the business people, so we need to make the best use of business law.

70 MIS

MANAGEMENT Information System (MIS) helps one to get pictures, graphs, pie charts, data, information, past records, present records, audit reports, videos, company information, annual reports, and much more. It captures large data, stores it in its data bank and it will be ready for use for future needs of the business enterprises. It uses some of the software tools, hardware tools, data, manpower, and certain rules and procedures, to make life easy for any business houses, business owners, and business management professionals.

MIS helps us to : get right information at the right time, computation works, decide, monitor things and control, provide training, to find and get the best manpower for your organizations and to move goods smoothly, for automation purposes, plan things, be competitive in the market, make profits, know strength and weakness of the organizations, get results quickly, to learn and relearn things, to be master of trade, to be master of business, build brand, to achieve great annual revenues, you can even learn things by using MIS and much more.

MIS is used in schools, colleges, universities, offices, SMEs, banks, insurance providers, governments, hyper markets, construction companies, infrastructure companies, factories or any business and educational setups.

By use of MIS everything everyday is on our finger tips. It can be any data, you get it in seconds by the use of computers. Colleges & schools can see data about their students of any year in seconds. It can be their pictures, their payments of fees, their report cards, their performance in subjects, exam results, etc. Companies can now find how many products are sold in the market just by sitting at their offices. MIS makes life easy for everyone.

You could even get total organization performance of any given day in seconds, so MIS makes one earn more profits and you could stay competitive in the market place.

MIS has seen many changes - computer to server, server to laptops, laptops to Wi-Fi, Wi-Fi to internet, internet to tablet and smart mobile phones.

MIS is for everyone and for every day so we need to make the best use of MIS.

71 Production Management

To convert materials into finished products, we need management that is Production Management. It included all the activities and efforts which are required to make a finished product. Production manager ensures all the finished goods are made in the factory right on time and he also takes responsibility of dispatching the goods from the factory to market place.

Production Management consists of : right organized planning, right movement of raw materials to the factory, vendor management, taking right decisions at the right time, ensuring all the production activities move freely and smoothly, cash management, budgeting, quality control, costing, achieving best finished product at low cost, right on time, time management, faster production.

A customer in the market place will never wait, he is on the go. So we need to ensure that our products are made available right on time and should also ensure that he buys our products. So all our energy, manpower, materials, machines, cash, plans, should not go waste, lot of time is spent by the factory men to make a finished product so we need to take great care of it.

Benefits of Production Management : Firms and companies can achieve their goals and objectives, more finished products, can venture into new businesses, can expand their business, can enter new markets, can increase their production capacity, can have better relationship with other firms, can build good relationship with their vendors, can Prosper, can get more profits, can achieve more sales in the market. "Produce first and be on the shelf firstâĂĺ, that is now we can produce faster and be in the market place much quicker than others. We can achieve competitive advantage, create goodwill, brand building, attain market leader position, support all other departments like marketing, HR, finance, systems, minimize cost of production, create more employment opportunities, build economy, can even double their production size, company gets bigger and bigger each day, contributes to country economic development, new Learning as we enter new technologies, employee satisfaction, Happy Company = Happy Employees.

Hence, Production Management is very crucial for any firm, so mange your activities, so that you save and increase your production and be a market leader. Higher your produce, more you sell in the market, and then there is more incoming profit for the firm. Isn't it interesting, cost of production for any product is getting expensive so we need to plan and produce and make higher profits.

72 Happy Employees Happy Company

For any company, its employees are the most important working assets, so we need to keep our employees happy everyday. There should be smile on employees face each day and every day, when they walk-in and walk-in out of the company they should be smiling and they should be happy, that's the great place to work, so we need to adopt all those practices where are employees stay happy. Smile is very attractive and good for health, employees will be fit to work, and company will be happy as their employees are contributing in a positive manner every day.

Smile brings in a new environment at work, smile make one stress free and relaxed, smile makes the body function at its best, smile makes you look young.

Employees join a company with great expectations, so it's our duty as a company to make their dreams come true. Definitely it should be mutually benefiting, so hire interested and like-minded employees who love your company, employees who love your company stay longer with the company. A relationship between the employee and the company is that of child and the parent, so we need to treat them like our family members, as they spend most of their time in the company working for us.

So welcome and greet your employees every day, make them responsible for their work, respect their views and work they get motivated and happy, get them some meals, some movie tickets, take them out, gift them a goody bag, they feel happy about the company, reward for their good work, train and place them, give them new learning opportunities at work, educate them about latest developments at work and the industry, motivate them to pursue higher education, promote them, hire a happy fun manager who keeps your employees happy all the time, create fun atmosphere, create indoor and outdoor games and allow them to play, coffee vending machines, tees, caps, theatre festivals, drama, music, entertainment programs from employees, cooking classes. Much more makes employees very happy, bring new ways and strategies to keep your employees happy, mentor them like your child.

Happy Employees = Happy Company

73 Leadership

LEADERSHIP is all efforts to lead a team or a group of people to achieve the companies goals and objectives. Leadership is making our employees realize about our dreams and aspirations, you has a company has many dreams, if you share them with the employees then employees will insert that in their blood and work accordingly. Country has produced the best leaders like Shri Ratan Tata, Shri Kumar Mangalam Birla, Shri Anil Ambani, Shri Mukesh Ambani, Shri Azim Premji, Shri Narayana Murthy and many others. All had great ideas and visions for their companies. They communicated them in front of their employees and the rest is history.

Leadership shows your employees new paths to achieve the goals of the company. It is definitely a collective task and all the employees should work united to achieve the task. They should volunteer and make the company bigger and bigger. To make the company happy, all employees should understand the company's dreams. Everyone should be responsible in their daily tasks and they should organize and keep little things ready and make sure they win the game. They should obey their managers, if you do not respect the manager then all goals will be not achieved. Small little contributions done by everyone can fetch great fruitful results to the company.

Leadership is all about wining the business games. For this our employees have to do preparation, planning, action, take necessary precautions, and also ensure they win the business game.

The best business plans and ideas will go in vain if not communicated well by the company leaders.

Employees should be honest, confident, committed, dedicated, enthusiastic and go getters. Employees make life easy for leaders if your leader is the best, if you hire a wrong leader at work then employees' work can go upside down.

So, you need to create the best working atmosphere to be a winner.

A leader should be creative, knowledgeable, goal oriented, winner, best communicator, positive attitude guy, sharing guy, thinker, caring, lovable, enthusiastic, action planner, 360 degree mapping expert, knowledge of industry, presenter, knowledge of market and competition, good teacher, friend and mentor, sportive in work, ability to inspire others and much more

Best leadership creates new landmarks and you can achieve great heights in business.

74 Mutual Funds

MUTUAL fund is an instrument where people can connect themselves and invest indirectly in stocks and bonds. It gives one complete knowledge of stock market for beginners and first time investors. It makes group of investors invest in various instruments like bonds, stocks, and other investments products. As an owner of the mutual fund, you will get your piece of share in units. All asset management companies work on behalf of their investors. Mutual fund companies have their own fund mangers. Fund managers make investors' life easy by doing research on stocks, bond, government bonds, securities. He studies business papers, business magazines, watches closely the movement of stock of all industries, and keeps all the information ready for use. He will work every day to give investors favorable returns. There are many companies today in the market like Birla Sun Life Mutual Fund, Edelweiss Mutual Fund, SBI Mutual Fund, HDFC Mutual Fund, Reliance Mutual Fund, HSBC Mutual Fund, IDBI Mutual Fund, Kotak Mahindra Mutual Fund, Motilal Oswal, etc.

Some benefits of Mutual Funds : Exposure to stocks and bonds, risk free, one will be knowledgeable, it makes life easy, you could even liquidate and get cash, easy entry and exit options for investors, tax advantages, future investment instrument, investors can now relax and watch their money grow and multiply, meets investors short term and long term financial goals, your fund manager gives assurances, you could start with Rs 500, money back, extra money which is lying in the bank is now in safe hands, better interest rates than banks and other products, if the stock market is in peak and one holds lot of diversified industry stocks then you could even get a lot of money, tension free - you do not have to watch your stock movements as fund managers take care of your stock and your money, secure investments, ready information 24/7, many people join you and invest along with you, you can be a proud owner of mutual fund, family members are now happy as you meet their future needs, money making machine, all time money, made for youth, middle aged, and old aged people, every one loves it.

So guys, go for Mutual funds for all your future needs.

75 Materials Management

MATERIALS management is movement of goods inside and outside the factory. Raw material comes in and finished goods go out of the factory, hence we need complete materials management. We need to move the raw materials to right places, store them, secure them, send them to production hubs. After the finished goods are done, we get to see a lot of junk and waste material lying at the factory premises. We need to keep hygiene at our factory, hence we need to move all the waste outside. Materials manager at the factory level ensures and plays with all the materials all day. He ensures raw materials are made available right on time, and also ensures that the factory premises is clean and in good conduction, inspection of all the raw materials, counting, trucks come in and go out of the factory, allocating trucks in order that there is smooth functioning, ensuring that production is happening 24/7. Without materials one cannot produce anything so management of materials is a must for all organizations.

Materials Management helps one : To store materials at right places, To move finished goods out of the factory, To Plan production, To Remove waste materials out of the factory, To Improve health and hygiene at factory, To get a clean environment, To get better working atmosphere, To recycle waste material, To route trucks, To load and Unload materials, To save fuel, power, idle time of trucks, To make green and eco friendly factory, To make short term production plans,

To achieve higher production, To save& make more profits, To reduce operating costs, To do emission testing, To do Quality Control, For R& D, Certification Like ISO, To make employees happy at factory, To make the best use of the available materials, To achieve economies of scale by making everything in order, Learn and Relearn, To know where things are right and wrong, To do landscaping at factory premises.

Hence, Material management is of great use to anyone who is in to production, or large scale manufacturing. Materials movement is very important, if all the materials are not there in time this could result in less profits. So if you need more goods to be produced at your factory, do materials management.

76 Show Business

Show Business in India is very big and happening. Some movies touche more than 100 crores & 200 crores today like the Bollywood movies Ghajini - Aamir Khan, Ek Tha Tiger - Salman Khan, & Chennai Express - SRK. 3 Khans have ruled the Bollywood industry for many years and have become big brands in the industry. People like to see them on screen first day first show. Indian cinema produces a lot of movies in all the languages. Some do well at the box office and some do average business. Today we could see many screens, many theatres, many multiplexes in major cities. Industry is big and happening, every year one gets to see new talent on screen. Industry has created a lot of direct and indirect jobs, whoever is associated with the show business has made a lot of money. We have some of the best studios and production houses in India. Some companies are using movies as their platform to showcase their brands. You could see brands even in movies, one can see clothing & fashion brands, cars, bikes, etc. One can even be a movie consultant and can do marketing for new movies. All you need to do is approach a producer with a marketing plan to promote the movie. India has produced best Bollywood, Kannada, Tamil, Telugu, Malayalam, Bengali, Punjabi movies, best directors, best actors, best producers, best technicians, best play back singers. India is the land of movies, so be in show business, entertain and make a lot of money.

The Show Business Market: Every Indian likes to see Indian cinema.

They eat, drink, sleep, watch only Indian cinema. So wherever you see Indians across the globe, there is market for Show Business. Today Indians have settled in many parts of the world, but they make sure they watch all the movies which are made in India. So now you can now find our Indian movies across the globe, isn't it interesting. So Show Business is huge, guys be in show business to entertain and to make a lot of money out there.

77 Fitness Industry - Six Packs Management

FITNESS is a state of being, where your body & mind functions at its best. You can go and do an extra mile in everything in your life, that is complete fitness. Fitness is an art where you program your mind to make your body look fit and healthy.

Some benefits of being fit : You feel happy about yourself, reduced stress - as we work 24/7 body and mind will be stressed, so exercises make you charged everyday, you look cool, energetic, fresh, muscular, charming, and others approach you, increased stamina, improves self confidence, reduces depression as now you stay focused in life, enjoy going out with others, reduces anxiety, your performance at work place improves every day, thereby you can contribute in a positive way for your company which you work, brain and heart and also overall body functions at it best, good memory power. You stay active all day, you stay organized in life, you make others protected from fear and also you make them happy, you start loving your own life, weight management - fat guys reduce weight, and lean guys put on some weight, you carry on with your customers well, you also inspire others - like the way Salman Khan did. He removes his shirt every time not to show off, but he inspires others to be fit. After he did so, everyone followed him in India. He was a mentor for others, he changed fitness industry. He is indirectly a positive contributor to Indian fitness industry. You will be creative at your task, you stay relaxed, you enjoy your sleep, you will take additional responsibilities at work place and at home. You start loving food, you will stop smoking, drinking and all kinds of additives in life. You live longer - life span improves, body skin improves, you read more - you start learning new things in life, it makes you educated. Being Fit is being a corporate rock star.

Being fit, cannot be achieved in one day, it is a dedicated and a planned approach in life. It is for you and only for you. So you have to program your exercises accordingly as per your needs. You have to do it regularly, and most important is you have to love it. Fitness will be gained over a period of time, it takes months, years to look fit. So guys hit the gym, run, jump, love exercises for complete fitness. Your employers start loving you for your fitness. Arnold Schwarzenegger is the God of body building and an Icon, he was Mr. Olympia seven times, a complete body building professional. He has inspired many across the globe, he is the terminator for millions in the world. His message to us is being fit, so guys be fit to face our day to day competitive world.

Fitness Industry today is on the peak. It is one of the most profitable businesses to be in. It has even created a lot of jobs in the market, like fitness consultant, coach, fitness trainer, diet planner, celebrity fitness trainer. One can even make a lot of money in this industry, just by helping others to be fit. There many popular brands in the market today, most poplar are Gold's Gym, Snap Fitness, Fitness One, Talwalkars and many others. If you are fit then you can stay active in life. Then you start bringing good results to your company, then you stay happy for rest of your life, so guys hit the GYM to be fit.

78 Love Cricket - Cricket Makes Us Not Out for Life

CRICKET is a happy super sport, all like to play or watch cricket. Children love playing cricket at young age, cricket is made to play for all age groups. Cricket makes you happy and cricket is an exciting game, cricket makes you Not Out for Life.

Companies' employees play cricket to show their power in business, to show their goals, every six show how employees achieve their goals. So cricket has to be practiced by companies to achieve greater heights in business.

Cricket makes one see your actions, plans, strategies, goals, objectives, aggressiveness, competiveness. Simple - what's there on your mind is on the score board, hence even in our day to day work places. 90 days hard work is out every quarter, all employees efforts will be visible in front of the public, so play hard and party harder like cricket.

Hence all companies should make a point to play cricket with their team members regularly.

Some benefits of playing Cricket : Cricket makes you fit, Cricket increases your stamina, Cricket makes you think, Cricket makes you flexible, Cricket makes you fast, Cricket improves your concentration, Cricket improves your strategic planning and implementation, Cricket improves your decision making skills, Cricket makes you disciplined in life, Cricket gives you opportunity to make new friends, as it a friendly game for all, Cricket makes you mentally fit, Cricket makes you responsible in life, Cricket tones your body, Heart will function all its best, Team building, Gives happy environment at work, Makes you Relax, You will be happy at home& at office and at play ground, Make you intelligent, Cricket make you adventurous, Cricket makes you jump, Cricket makes you love your life, Cricket builds new relationships, Cricket brings in more profits, Cricket makes you lovable, Cricket gives Happy Companies and Happy Employees. There are many benefits by playing cricket, so guys go out with your cricket bat and ball, and play cricket to be happy all day, and to bring happiness to our companies which you work for.

Cricket makes you Not Out for life.

79 Luxury Brand Management

Gucci, Armani, Louis Vinton, Jimmy Choo. So many brands have entered the Indian luxury market and some are on the way. Indian luxury market is growing every year, as there is a lot of demand and lot of potential customers who like to buy these products. There is a demand for luxury brand management professionals in the areas of brand building, sales and marketing, merchandising, etc. India is a super rich Country, you find higher percentage of super rich people in India, super rich like to shop for expensive goods which suits their interest from chocolates, wines, watches, jewellery, custom made cars, high end cars, pens, perfumes, high end expensive luxury apartments and villas, spa, cosmetics treatments, dental treatments, leather goods, fashion accessories, and much more.

In the next 5 years, there will be many international players in the Indian luxury market. Foreign visitors are on the rise, so luxury market has to even cater to foreigners, so presence of luxury market is important. Luxury goods should be made available freely both for Indians and foreigners and upper middle class. Rich like to shop for more luxury brands, earnings of individuals have gone up in India, they have high disposable income, super rich like to spend on buying luxury goods, so demand for luxury brands is on the rise. We even have luxury malls like UB city in Bangalore. You can find international brands in UB City, there are already established brands, existing brands and growing international brands in India, some luxury brands are doing really well.

Luxury Brand Management course is very interesting and highly rewarding. One gets knowledge of all international brands in the market, their heritage and much more. After the course, one can make strategy, sell well and build brands. There are some professional courses in luxury brand management in India. You could even go abroad to do this course. Compensation packages vary from brand to brand. At entry level you could start at a good higher package, and a lot of incentives, perks, food, foreign travel, and the best part of this business is you get to meet and know super rich guys, celebrities and HNI, all drop in to your store. Hence the more you sell, bigger will be your annual package.

Luxury Brand management is creating a new market for the elite class. Selling the products to potential customers, bigger higher revenue to the company, and build brand, and also taking care of the brand image well. Usually a Luxury Brand Manger is responsible for all the sales, marketing and brand building for a particular international luxury brand. He or she can also specialize in some core products like apparel, fashion, foot wear, accessories, spa, reality and much more. All pay well and all come with great respect and higher compensation package and with great responsibility. You can work in India, or you can also work abroad as a luxury brand manager. MBA in Luxury Brand Management with International Brands experience can make you move around the world .

International Luxury Brand Managers responsibilities : Making a Business Plan and presenting it to the top management, Making the Business Plan work and achieving it, Directing Sales to consultants at store, Merchandising, Training the Staff members, Marketing, Visual Merchandising, Advertising, Brand building, Ensuring all the rules are in place, Maintaining optimum stock levels, Increasing sales every week and every month, Increasing overall profits, Reducing un necessary expenditures, Theft Management, People Management, Stock Management, Observing competitors moves, Store operations, Time management, Stress management, Customer Management, Customization, Designing, Handling multiple clients at times, Handling Queries.

Super cool job as a Luxury Brand Manager, so guys go for it and sell international brands to rest of the world.

80 Business Ethics

Business Ethics are rules and codes set by the management, this is applicable to all the employees of the organization to carry out their business activities ethically.

In today's hard realities of business world, we face many challenges from the outside world. Yet whatever may be the hard realities, we should be ethical in all our business activities. Ethics should be in our blood, because one can achieve only short term goals, by being unethical, but definitely one cannot practice it every day for long, If you do it regularly, your business does not last long. First management has to be ethical, then they should frame codes and principles for all to follow in an organization. All employees should be informed to have a ethical approach in their daily business activities. Even today big giant companies are very successful, only because that they are ethical in their business activities.

Ethics means making right products without comprising on quality, pricing the product right and not to over price to make short term profits, no bribes - you should not give money, kind or do favors to anyone to get a business deal, or to push products in the market. Maximizing of the profits should be done ethically. Earning good name in the market takes years, but losing and taking a bad name takes seconds, so be ethical in all your business activities.

Tata group is a living example for being country's best ethical and most trusted business house. Customers, stake holders, general public, investors, Tata Group employees are proud to have association with Tata group. All employees at Tata group follow Tata code of conduct. By this all their business activities will be carried out easily and smoothly with great care without any complaints, that is the beauty of being Tata's.

Ethical behavior makes you grow bigger and bigger, and unethical behavior can make you out of the market, choice is ours.

Some benefits of being ethical in our business activities : Clean Business Environment, Social Responsibility, Quality Products and Services, Government respect you as you are transparent in your business and you pay your taxes on time, You will be a role model to others in the market, You will be smart company, Organization will be in healthy condition, Happy Employees Happy Company, Transparent and Open for new learning, You will be Cool Company, You will be traditional yet modern, Company's heritage will be protected, Good Work Environment, More Incoming Cash and Profits, Vendors are happy to supply raw materials to you, as their payments are on time, Share holders will earn more dividends and share prices will be growing every year, Customers will be happy to purchase products from shelf Example : Tata Nano, Tata Tea, It builds brands, You get good market coverage and Reach, Society respect you, Associations respect you and you will be awarded, All admire you, You will be a Winner, You will achieve all you have dream of, Mission and Vision will be achieved, Overall you be powerful.

So many benefits, of being ethical, so be ethical, please remember one thing, the biggest spy camera is God, we can get away easily from anyone but not with the God, so guys be ethical in all your business activities.

81 Business Environment

Business environment is the area in which business enterprises operate. It consists of suppliers, customers, distributors, substitute products in the market place, competitors, products and services in that industry, brands, rules and regulations of that particular industry, industry dynamics, government agencies, economical trends, new technological developments, demography, labor, natural resources and raw materials, business plans, social and cultural factors, political influences, future trends of that particular industry, growth opportunities, production rules, labor laws, unions, government support to that industry. Hence we find that business areas in which we operate consists of so many factors, all these and much more constitute the business environment.

Business environment study helps : one to plan things better, one to introduce right products and services and also the right pricing for products and services, one to build good relationships with who ever associated in their business, one to make strategic moves and face the competition, one to add value to your products and services, one to build brands, One to earn good reputation in the market, one to carry on their business activities well every day, one to do SWOT (Strength, Weakness, Opportunities, and Threats) analysis, and also helps one to take appropriate measures and actions, one to carry future course of actions, one to produce right products and increase production capacities, one to maintain a healthy working environment, one to maintain coordinal relationship with everyone, onee to increase profits every day and also helps one to make their company bigger and better, one to conduct suitable training programs for their employees, one to be good pay masters, one to introduce right and suitable new technologies at work, one to Learn and Relearn, one to know their industry well, onee to follow as per government rules and regulations, one to plan for their taxes, one to adopt time management, one to make their employees happy, wealthy, knowledgeable& healthy, one to make a Happy Company, one to establish itself as a great company, one to stay long in business.

In today's business, we need to have a knowledge of our business environment to stay long and make a lot of profits.

82 Wealth Management

WEALTH Management is all about multiplying wealth and finding ways and means and sources to increase wealth for others, that is wealth management.

Today we have professionals in this trade, there are also professional certifications like certified financial planner. One learns the art of increasing wealth by investing in various financial tools. It can be in stock markets, mutual funds, estate planning, bonds, insurance, and other investments. Wealth Manager is responsible in giving complete guidance to their prospective clients. Investors get full information on various investments from their wealth managers. There are many wealth management companies operating in India. All companies are using their best strategies to increase the wealth of their clients. Any investors will be definetly benefitted by taking suitable guidance from their wealth managers. Wealth mangers will also makes a lot of wealth for himself, so it is the best business to be in, because it is all about multiplication of wealth. Industry has created a lot of jobs. If one is interested, one can get into wealth management solutions business. But wealth management comes with great responsibility, because the investors have put in lot of money & they have trusted their respective wealth management companies.

So wealth managers have to keep up to their standards of their investors. Once the investors lose trust then you lose many other businesses. So this business comes with great responsibility, so do continuous research and understand your markets well to perform well in this trade.

So guys start multiplying wealth for others and for yourself.

83 Talent Management

Some talented people are gifted and are sent by God for a purpose for the benefit of the society, and some talents are made by schools, colleges, and at companies, so talent is a bank full of rich knowledge, new ideas, mission, and much more, so all companies should make the best use of their talented people, talent should be nurtured everyday, talent is cash.

Example - An IIM Grad, after he joins the company, the company looks powerful, both inside and outside, main reason of talent in house, because he brings in rich collection of ideas, management fundas, knowledge transfer from his professors at classrooms, work experience and much more. Don't you think this guy will be a great asset to the company, you could see him in action in his internship, and them also at work, they bring in change, new growth in the company, so having a talent is like having a new bank account with lots of bank balances, so we need to make the best use of the available talent in house, we need to take special care of them, give them best compensation packages, and with all facilities, if the talent remains with the organization for long, then the companies can make a lot of profits.

Happy Talent Management

84 Training & Development

Training is a must for all. It makes you learn about the company, industry, departments, competition. Training is a purpose to achieve the goals of the company, so one as to learn to work and to perform well in the company. It is good for overall career development and for the overall growth of the company, so go training, example to work on SAP software we need training on SAP. Training makes you strong and confident to handle any business situations. As and when company ventures into new business, one require training, so training prepares to face you from day to day challenges in the market. There will be fast technological developments in the market on has to learn them quickly to stay a head of the competition, and one can also perform like Rock Stars.

Practical Example : We never had computers, laptops, software packages, mobiles, tabs in the past, we learnt it. So learn everything to perform well at your work place. Training activities cost a lot of money, so we need to make the best use of training and HR department should give trainings on things which they can apply fast at work. So customize your training needs for the benefit of all.

Development - An employee cannot stay the way he is for years. He has to change, he needs growth that's development. He or she has to grow along with the organization. So all companies should ensure that they develop new skills and grow along with the organization.

Development is moving up to the next levels, it applies to both organization and its employees. So develop yourself along with your companies & bring in new changes and higher profits.

85 Corporate Image Management

Corporate Image is like an identity of a company in general public. A customer, public at large, investors, suppliers, creditors, shareholders, all have great expectations from the company. So it is up to the management to lay down fundamentals to present itself as a good corporate in front of everyone. This requires good management, if you project yourself bad, its negative for the company, and if you do good and all respect your company, that's the pure meaning of Corporate Image Management.

HUL, Coca Cola, Pepsi, Nestle, MTR, Tata Motors, Tata Global Beverages, Tata Chemicals, TCS, Titan, Tata Sons, Tata Housing, Tata Capital, Reliance, Aditya Birla, Arvind Mills, Nokia, Samsung, BHEL, BEML, etc. all are big names in the industry today and all have good corporate image in general public. They have taken years to build trust among the people, by giving quality good and services, best work practices, best employees and they have wined the hearts of millions of customers in India.

Just imagine you are a top corporate in India. Now let's go to the market and let's do a market research and ask the public names of atleast 25 best corporates in India, and if they recall your company then you are the best. Then if they cannot recall your company then you have to take suitable measures. A company which is in the minds and hearts of the Indian masses has a good corporate image in the market.

Corporate image cannot be build in just one day. It takes years to build good relationship with everyone, that's with the customer, suppliers, governments, tax authorities, law, vendors, creditors, stake holders, general public, advertising agencies, market research firms, banks and financial institutions, and all whoever is associated with the corporate. So all our actions will fetch good corporate image.

Sum of all corporate actions is equal to a good corporate image. If you remember your spiderman movies, one character in one of the movie is black spider for few minutes. Look at the way the image of the spiderman is destroyed because it is projecting itself as negative. So if a corporate does negative actions you can be upside down, so be responsible for your super powers, that is corporate image management.

Good Corporate image can be achieved by : Being Good, By having a emotional bonding with the customer, Human touch principle, Care for all, By providing quality good and services,By designing best logo where a customer recalls the logo - example apple phones and computers, Good messages, Best Advertising, By Being Socially Responsible, Well Managed, Research Oriented, Dedicated Employees, Good Relationship with all, Fair and transparent in all the business deals, Right communication flow, Being Ethical, Maintaining good rapport with all, Regular auditing in all departments, 360 degree effort from everyone in the organization, Hard work, Smart work, Lovable, By introducing new innovative products, New methods of working, By adapting to new technologies, Making everyone happy.

Corporate Image Management gives you higher profits and you stay long in the market, so manage you brands, logo, your people, be responsible for everything you do.

86 Management Consulting

MANAGEMENT Consulting is an expert advice and a perfect knowledge transfer by management consultants to accelerate business. We can now move the business to next level and it helps one to achieve greater heights in business and make huge profits.

Some benefits of management consulting are : They are experts in the industry and they give us road map for the future. They scan both internal and external environments. They conduct SWOT analysis of the firm. They analyse present business situations. They will solve present business problems. They will improve current business performance. They work with all departments like HR, Marketing, IT, Finance, Administration, Security, Transport, Logistics, Production, etc and understand and give solutions to each department. They work 24/7 and around the world. They have clientele across the globe. They love to see their companies as winners. They create future leaders. They adopt best tools and practices. They bring in best strategies, give accurate future predictions of your business. They do research and give you answers. They make our employees super performers. They suggest suitable course of actions. They help the firm in designing the best logo, punch line, they make the brands heard in the market place. They give us best marketing and action plans. They are specific and goal oriented. They bring in more profits, best policies and practices at work. They train our employees well. All knowledge transfer from them is a purpose that will change and bring in a overall organizational development. They create winning super companies. Their charges are not all that expensive, as it is time bound and short term, and it is one time payment. They give us best employees who will run the show.

Management consulting is the best method for any company because they analyze present company situations and will give us best methods, they customize solutions as per client requirements - the man who gives expert advice and solve business problems, and makes the show go on, is called Management Consultant.

87 Negotiation

NEGOTIATION is an art of winning situations, what's there on your mind you win or you bring it in paper, that's negotiation. You actually make the opposite person agree to your terms and conditions, which are mutually beneficial. So plan what you what from the deal, never be hurry, relax, be calm and silent, listen carefully, understand the terms, understand the nature of the deal, fix your targets, be right all the time, do research, and get the best deal.

Some benefits from negotiation : You enter new businesses, Helps you grow, Helps you enter new markets, You get an opportunity to join hands with other business heads, You make more profits, You be happy and satisfied, You learn new things, You get to see new technologies, You Share knowledge, resources, talent with others and make money, You get recognition, Overall development of the business, You get new land, and resources, You party hard as you win, It will build new brands, It builds nations, Wining Situations, Existing new opportunities, You go global, You be now dynamic in nature, You be now work alcoholic, You will be a winner, You will be successful, You will be powerful, You will become business leader, You stay focused, You will be happy and relaxed.

80 % of the deals are closed by investing quality time on research and preparation before going for negotiation.

88 Quality Management Systems

QUALITY Management is a continuous activity by everyone in the organization, to achieve the goals of the organizations. We bring in best policies, practices, procedures, objectives in place. We also ensure we follow these set of rules, we also review then at a regular basis. By all these one achieves quality in all departments, quality in work, quality products. Quality management itself is an effort to make a company the best in its class. One gets relevant certification after the quality management audit, which is issued by the concern authorities, for example our ISO certification.

Some benefits of Quality Management Systems are : Organized activities in all departments, Everyone in the organization stay focused, Everyone in the organization stay active, Out Put = Quality Goods and Services, Employees are now well trained, Flow of communication is smooth in the entire organization, One gets a perfect reporting structure, All employees are now more responsible towards their work, Resources will be well managed, Cost cutting measures, Helps one to do bench marking with others in the industry, New methods and procedures in place, New actions plans very quarter for all departments is now ready, Monitoring becomes easy, International Recognition and Quality Management Certification, Increased efficiency at work, Reduce costs, Minimizes risk and damages, World wide acceptance, More sales, More incoming cash, You meet the needs of consumers at market place, consumer is happy, Saves time, Faster reach, consumers will get products now on time, Quality customer service, New business growth and new existing opportunities.

So, benefits of quality management systems are more, so one has to go for quality management systems to achieve new heights in business, and earn respect in the industry with they operate.

89 Business Ideas

An Idea can transform your life, so guys if you want to be a free bird and if you are talented, hard working, go getter, dedicated, hunger for money, and if you have a special concern for society and people, then business is the right option. To do business you need a idea, so develop a business idea and start up.

These are some business ideas one can start with low investments : Coffee Tea House - You could sell coffee tea packs and also serve hot and cold coffee tea with snacks, Plant more trees - sell plastic and ceramic pots to homes and offices - tie up with a nursery, Car washing at door steps, Online Grocery Store - free home delivery, Fresh Fruits and Vegetables - Home delivery, Home made chocolate store, Home made ice-cream store, Education Consulting - world wide, Corporate Gifts - Customized gifts for your employees, Candle Making, Event management, T-shirt print with unique messages, Human Resource Consulting world wide, Dance and Music Studio, Gym& Yoga Studio, Travel Solutions world wide, Online customized fashion studio, Rent a Car and Bike, Home made food, Home Delivery, Seconds Electronic Super Store, Rent Books, Flyer Distribution for different brands, Online Used Car Showroom, Tutoring Services, Art Studio, Short term Self defense training for Women.

First choose your industry, then choose products or service business then make a idea, then start up.

90 Operations Research

Operations Research, as the name suggests, is an operation to find solutions from business problems, after continuous research we get right data, we use these collected data samples to our best of our abilities for decision making in business. Operations Research gives you Google map view of a business problem, there by we work hard to get solutions.

Some of the benefits from Operation Research : Helps One can get to know the current business standing, and we can also get to know what when wrong and how to rectify the same, also helps us in decision making, Helps one to gather right data for future use, Helps one to make a Strategic move in the market, Helps one to get a bird's eye view of the industry and growth prospects, Helps on to solve short term and long term business problems, Helps one to do a complete research in one area, Helps one to do advanced study, Helps one to do knowledge transfer, Helps one to get new existing business opportunities, Helps one to reduce the cost of operation, Helps one to find new working methods, Helps one to get new directions in business, Helps one to achieve business objectives, Helps one to achieve new heights in business, Helps one to produce quality goods, Helps one to increase production capacities, Helps one to make the best use of resources, Helps one to manage time well, Helps a Sales person to be organized, there by he travels more, time taken to travel is less, and there by he brings more orders to firm, Helps one to focus, Helps one to be a powerful in business, Helps one to build more brands, Helps one to make their consumers happy in the market, Helps one to make their employees happy and satisfied, Helps one to make more profits from business, Helps one to grow in business every day.

Benefits of Operations Research are many, because it gives a firm quality solutions to problems and also helps in decision making.

91 Work Experience

THEORY knowledge makes one know about industry, competitors, different subject knowledge, products and services, brands, economics, business, ideas. But your real application of knowledge happens only when you start working for others.

So work experience is very important. You face live challenges on a daily basis at your work place, your learning does not end here, it is a continuous process. So one acquire knowledge even at their work place, so guys go out and work for others.

Some benefits of work experience are : One develops new skills sets, One gets new fresh experience, Helps one to choose the line of business, You get opportunities to work with teams, Great Learning Opportunities, One can develop managerial skills, You stay confident and motivated, You improve your communication skills, as we speak to everyone at work and customers, You get to know live business understanding of your chosen sector or industry, You can pursue higher education along with your work, You understand ethical principles in business, One learns how to talk to different people, customers, handling telephone, sending mails, organizing meetings and much more, Helps one to contribute to the company and its industry, One starts bringing new changes in the company, by giving suitable suggestions, One find new methods of working, Overall development of personality, One stays happy, as there pockets are now full, because of salary and perks You could get mentors and friends for life time, Resume is now rich and has weight in it, Full practical Live Business Theatre - is your work Place, You add more skills, Career advancement, Adds new competencies, Helps for one future, Increase in compensation package, Solid foundation for the future, you can even work or you can start on your own after your work experience.

Work experience is like a mirror, when one looks at it you get to know what strengths you have to face the business challenges in a daily basis. It shows how much worth one is. It makes you employed, it gives you money, happiness. It is easy to take people with experience because you have readymade skills, one can hit the market from day one, that's the beauty of having work experience.

92 Business Icons

I am proud to be an Indian, because India is very rich in natural resources, opportunities, and highly educated people. I have grown seeing, visiting, and working with one of best companies in India. Business icons have not only just created big houses, companies, brands in the market, but have also created millions of job opportunities for others. They have utilized the opportunity and they have made it big. They are classy cool, super rich, powerful, highly educated business professionals, big contributors to the nation. Business leaders and icons have made crorepatis along with them, simply because Indian people also trusted in their business plan and have joined hand with them. They had a dream, they worked hard with best of their abilities, they have made super India today.

Some business Icons : JRD Tata, Ratan Tata - Tata group, Kumar Mangalam Birla - Aditya Birla Group, Dhirubhai Ambani - Reliance, Mukesh Ambani - Reliance Industries, Anil Ambani - Anil Dhirubhai Ambani Group, Azim Premji - Wipro, Adi Godrej - Godrej Group, Anand Mahindra - Mahindra & Mahindra, Kishore Biyani - Future Group, Naveen Jindal - Jindal Group, Laksmi N Mittal - Arcelor Mittal.

In India we have great business people, with super ideas they have made it big for themselves and for everyone, even in bollywood - Salman Khan, Aamir Khan, Shahruk Khan are also like business icons. They are producing best movies for India and have also created jobs, in India. Thousands of people register themselves has proprietors, partnership firms, private limited,etc. everyone likes to be big and famous. Being in business is a great responsibility, so one has to be dynamic and should know how to manage resource, and create jobs, create best products and services, and if people like it then the rest is the history. I personally encourage everyone to be in business, because you make money, name, and you create jobs and your friends and family love you. Today we see many start-ups with small capital, then they are big one day, example myntra.com.

Business Icons are powerful and have made India proud, so it's time for us to startup on our own, build a brand and serve our nation - planet India.

93 Raw Materials

Raw materials knowledge is a must for all, because one gets to know various types of raw materials and also its pricing. To do business, raw materials knowledge will be very useful, any business person or a purchase manager should have sound knowledge of raw materials and its daily price movements in the market. He should be in constant touch with the vendors and information should be on his finger tips to conduct his daily business activities.

Let us take an example of textile manufacturing - important component in manufacturing a garment is material and its material cost, so that we can make a finished garment, we need materials like fabric, tags, labels thread,etc.

First step is that we make a list of materials required to make a finished product, then its prices, then prepare costing.

Case Study : Lets us assume a corporate gifting company has bagged a big order to supply polo t-shirts with MTR company logo printed on t-shirts. They had given a quotation to supply and they got 5,000 t-shirts order to supply, price per t-shirts is 300 Rupees. Bad luck, ministry has increased the raw materials. Now the price of cotton, yarn, knitting, dyeing, thread, buttons & labels has gone up, corporate gifting firm hastaken 50 % advance from their client. What is the immediate reaction from the corporate gifting firm and the delivery is within 15 days.

Think Positive : Purchase Manager of corporate gifting company has already made arrangement in his factory. He blocked all raw materials two days ago and hence t-shirts can be produced at the same cost.

This case study explains us how raw materials and its prices can bring changes in your business. So have a watch on the market, raw materials prices and their movements. Good information can make you wealthy and no knowledge can make one out of the market. So be prepared for actions. The same is applicable to any product or any industry.

Raw materials knowledge helps one to do business easily, helps one to produce more, helps one to have edge in the market, helps one to plan their production activities, helps one to produce at low cost, helps one to make more profits, helps one to achieve company's objectives, we can produce and offer products to end consumer at best prices.

Raw materials knowledge is also helps a consumer as now he buys at products at right prices from the market.

So guys, raw material knowledge will be very useful to everyone. It can be for making shirts, trousers, pizzas, biryani, masala dosa, idli, vada, sambar, and to a automobile car maker, or even for constructing a home or an apartment every one needs raw material knowledge for their future use and business requirements.

94 Around the World - Tourism Industry

Toursim sector in India, today is on its peak, as we have millions of domestic and international foreign visitors. Indian tourism sector earns a lot of money from its visitors. India is rich, colorful, traditional, rich value based citizens. One gets to have a variety of food, lots of interesting places in all corners of India, festivals, different cultures, best unique clothing boutiques, best hotels, best transport facilities, best companies, and very economical holiday destination compare to other foreign destinations.

People in India respect and love one another and they also respect their foreign visitor too. We find holiday advertisement in leading newspaper from tourism service providers. In India one can find a lot of interesting places to visit, more visitors, and thereby it generates a lot of revenue for everyone whoever is associated with tourism industry.

Some famous tourist destination in India - Taj Mahal - Agra, Simla - Hill Station, Ooty - Hill Station, Kashi Temple - Varanasi, Mumbai - Business Capital, Bangalore - Best Weather, Mysore - Palace, Zoo, Temples and more, Chennai - Automobiles and food, Coorg - Wildlife and Food, Goa - Beaches, apart from all these we have best malls, fashion boutiques, food courts, best street food across India. One needs a life time to cover India, all corners of India have best places to visit.

Best tourist service providers in India- MakemyTrip, Thomas Cook, Cox & Kings, Yatra, SOTC, Goibibo, Expedia, Clear Trip, Travel guru, Mahindra Holidays, all offer world class domestic and international travel services, holiday packages, best hotel reservations, shopping tours, flight, train, bus reservation facilities, travel insurance, foreign exchange, corporate travel facilities, wildlife tours, world wide office network, car rentals, customized holidays.

Tourism sector has created a lot of jobs and business opportunities to millions in India. If you are a graduate with good communication skills, you could work in any of the famous brands. They offer high compensation packages, it can be in booking a ticket, organizing tours, guides, photographers, hotel reservations, car rentals, franchisees. Whoever is associated with the word 'tourism in India', makes a lot of money, because of its visitors. So one has to take special care of visitors. More visitors = More money = Growth in tourism industry. If one is keen to work in this industry, he or she has to be passionate and should love travelling. Industry service providers has to take special care, love and affection, attention, guide tourists well, it applies to both domestic and foreign visitors, we should respect everyone.

Around the world we have some of the famous destinations like : Taj Mahal - India, Mysore Palace - India, Pyramids of Giza - Egypt, The Vatican City - Rome, Statue of Liberty - New York, Eiffel Tower - Paris, Great wall of China, Disney land Park - USA, the list goes on and on.

The World is filled with best destinations, so much to see, so guys let us pack our bags and let us go see the world.

95 Bulls & Bears - Understanding Stock Markets

Bulls - If the market is on the top, market is on the rising mood, bulls are active, market has more buyers than sellers in stock market. Bears - If the market tends to fall gradually, weak market, less buyers and many sellers, bears are active, falling mood of stock market.

Bull is good because it gives you good return on investments, short term profits. But one cannot under-estimate a bear market. Even if the market is low, share prices are low and is easy to pick stocks, one can sell them when the market swings upside.

They are various factors which affect the stock market like economy, employments, industry growth, buyers and sellers moods, FDI, government, politics, business conditions, and much more. Stock Exchange helps one to buy and sell stocks, one can buy and sell if and only if it is listed in the stock exchange. Bombay Stock Exchange and National Stock Exchange are the two biggest stock exchanges in India. Stock Market is open for all investors. It is risky, challenging, volatile, but still it gives you best returns. One has to open a demat and trading account to start buying and selling of stocks in the stock market. You can go to your nearby franchisee or a broker to open your accounts. You need simple documents like pan card, identity proof, cancelled cheque, bank account, bank statements. You will be happy to see your money grow with the help of your accounts.

Some stock trading companies : ICICI Direct, Share Khan, 5 Paisa,

Motilal Oswal Securities, Reliance Money, Kotak Securities. You can drop in to their offices to open your accounts, or if you call them they will send their representative at your homes. They open your Demat and Trading Accounts, they offer stock trading services, e-trading, live stock updates, market research, merchant banking, trading tips, chat, investment banking, depository services, portfolio management, fixed income, broking services, bonds, mutual funds, forex, commodities.

Money does not multiply in one day, it takes some time. So one has to put in time, energy, do quality research on stock markets and stocks, have a good portfolio of stocks, a stock broker helps one to build good portfolio. One should also read books on stock market, business newspaper & magazines, invest in long term and get fruitful returns, make your own strategy and action plans before investing in stock markets, invest wisely and regularly.

Dematerialized - Demat - shares and securities will be in your account in electronic form. In olden days we had physical certificates but now it's demat. Even your bonuses are directly credited to your account, you get settlement easily, it's easy and fast. A small percentage of your money goes as brokerage to service providers.

There are millions of people in India, who have become crorepatis by investing in stock market. A small investment 20 years back in stock market is now worth millions. Investors who had invested money in stocks like HUL, Infosys, Wipro, Titan, Banking Stocks, IT, Pharmaceuticals, Automobile in the past has fetched great returns. India has created a lot of job opportunities, whosoever is associated with Stock Markets, it can be a broker, franchisee holder, investors, companies, all have made good money. If you like to make money for yourself and others, it's a right place to work or to do business. So guys be a long term investor, and enjoy all the wealth made from stock market.

Happy Trading

96 Franchisee Business

FRANCHISEE business is the easiest way to be in business, because everything is just ready, from business name, business model, equipments, choosing a location, stocks, till manpower, almost everything is ready to run the show. All you need to do is have passion, interest in business and investment in franchisee business. In return of investment made, one can make a lot of money.

They are different types of franchisee models in the markets across industry like food and beverages, hotels and resorts, retail, fashion, boutique, health and fitness, jewellery business, manufacturing, financial services education, manufacturing, media and advertisements.

Investments vary from company to company, brand to brand. It starts from Rs 10,000 and goes up to 5 Crores rupees. It depends on the business you choose to be in. Franchisee made one to be on his own, you can be proud to say that I am a franchisee owner. Training is given by the company which you work for, company is also benefitted by having more outlets and hubs across different locations and cities. If you do not like it, you can even exit from the franchisee business, it is that easy.

Some popular franchisee names - US Polo, Flying Machine, Lee, Spykar, Levis, Pepe, Mr & Mrs Idly, McDonald's, Subway, Domino's Pizza, Café Coffee Day, Raymonds, World of Titan, Fastrack,& the list goes on and on.

Lets us see how franchisee model gives us great returns :

Example : Famous Clothing Brand

Franchisee Investment - 50-60 Lakhs

Min Store Requirements - 1000 sq ft space either own building/leased/rental

Area - High Foot Fall Street/Malls

Minimum expenditure every month : Rental has to be borne by the franchisee, electricity, water, telephone, internet, and all fixed expenses have to be borne by the franchisee holder.

Company support : Manpower, merchandising, branding, interiors, lighting, fixtures and furniture, stock will take back unsold garments, 30 % Profit for franchisee on MRP, marketing and sales support, regular visits from company officials and time to time support.

I am interested now to take up this franchisee, made a total investment of 50 lakh rupees after negotiations and even the rent is now borne by the company. Now I still get 30% profit. Company has projected a minimum sale of 1 crore in one year. In five years it will be 5 crores, that is 1.5 crore rupees incoming cash to franchisee. Franchisee makes one to have cash in pockets on a daily basis and can be very wealthy if you continue in business. Easiest way to double your money is by having multiple franchisees.

Every year we have franchisee expo so if you guys want to take up franchisee of a company, it is the right place to be in.

Happy Franchisee

97 Merger & Acquisition

IN an industry, we find common producers. Producer X is into ready to eat snacks packs. He is well organized and is getting more orders from the market and now likes to increase his production capacities. He is already an established player in the market. Now he meets Producer Y, who is also into similar business, but they are looking for partners. Now producer X and producer Y merges itself and now jointly they have 2 production units, manpower support, investments, market coverage, technologies, products and brands.

Now producer X takes full charge and control of all the activities. Acquisition is simply purchasing a another company.

Some benefits of M& A : It is like getting married to someone and taking full responsibility, adds more production capacities, volumes increases, Adds new technologies, adds new systems and processes, Adds new talented work force, Team work, Makes one a market leader, Makes one powerful, Makes one Rich and Powerful, Helps one to maintain dominant position in the market, Adds new Challenges, Adds new Strategies, Cost efficient, reduced cost, Better Market Coverage, Adds more products and Brands, More Sales Orders, Adds Competencies.

Suppliers are happy to supply goods, Investors are happy, Customers are now happy, as they get new products in hand, can venture into more businesses, adds value to the company, Builds reputations in the market, Brings more incoming cash, Brings more happiness.

M& A brings so many benefits, it's a complete value addition to the acquiring company.

98 Go Getter

Life is full of challenges. Every day we get up in the morning we have a list of tasks to do. We have to get it at any cost and at the same time we get few more challenges by the afternoon. So we have so much to do and we have only 10 working hours & we have to get it all and we have to get it right.

If you are like a go getter, everyone likes you, everyone respect you for the work done. Believe me in a human life, we have to achieve so many things for ourselves, others, parents, company which we work for, kids, loved ones, most important our Country India.

So how to achieve so many things in a short span of life, answer is simple be a Go getter.

Go getter is winning, what is there in your mind, if you program it, you will definitely achieve it.

To program it you need right knowledge and good preparation.

At the same time one should be passionate enough, and the mental state of mind should be to get things done.

So what is knowledge and preparation ?

Knowledge is information about the task to achieve, it can be a game, it can be a sales target, it can be making short term profits in stock market, it can be getting deals in place, wining a war.

1. Example 1 : In archery, my target is bull's eye, to do that I need to know the history of archery. How to make a bow and arrow

myself, how to make a bull's eye, and see some videos, and then practice for 100 days. Then you are on the go to hit the bull's eye.

2. Example 2 : Ghajini - the man himself, Aaamir Khan, the super Star in Bollywood. To do the movie Ghajini, Aaamir Khan had to be completely fit and active. He hit the gym and made himself look stronger, powerful, and muscular, it came well on screen as well. The result was it entered 100 crore club, Aaamir Khan is a go getter.

3. Example 3 : Area Salesmanger - FMCG, has a target of 300 crores this year. He has one sales officer and 30 territory sales in charge, and also has distributor salesmen. He looks after entire Karnataka Region, India. Now he calls his team meet in Bangalore. All are present, now the planning and preparation, he gives individual targets to everyone. He also allocates their territories, he also motivates them with good incentives and career growth in the company for performers. Now he gives them daily chart, weekly chart, monthly chart, quarterly chart, and yearly chart. He clearly explains how many orders have to be taken per day and them multiplies it, so the task is now easy. Now sales force is ready to hit the market and all are going with the go getting attitude.

So have a dream, set targets for yourself, 'I want to get this for me'. It can be an MBA entrance Exam like CAT, IAS competitive exam, sales targets, buying a car, villa or an apartment for your family, & then prepare and plan and go get it.

Go getters will be happy all day, they make others also happy. So be a go getter.

99 Racing

Past is Past, now we have the present with us and we need to make the best use of it. So live every day as a race day, every second is precious and valuable in our lives. From morning to night we meet many competitors, all likes to win the game of life, so prepare, plan, and go racing.

Go racing simply means, one has to be super-fast in their daily activities. Organize things well for yourself, live up to everybody's standards, & win the game. Set targets for yourself, & go racing like a super hero. One's objective must be to attain the number one position in the market in whatever we do. It can be academics, teaching, learning, at jobs, at business, one has to be number one. At business level, everyone has to meet their deadlines, people like racers, so go racing. If you go to any sports competition, you find many racers - it can be running, swimming, jumping, formula one race, all are on the go, and all eyes are on one person, that's the winner. So we need to be winners and not losers. Racing is a purpose in life, if one does not win the game, he or she will not be happy. Someone out there is waiting for us, so for them we need to be winners. God has made everyone like super heroes and to be winners, he has given all necessary basic needs and resources, so we need to utilize all these and be winners. God has sent mentors also that's our parents and teachers who help us to be winners, so what are you waiting for go racing.

Even in real life situations, investors like winners, everyone likes to invest on winners only, that's the reality of life, so go racing, think that today is your last day, and have target before you leave home, you will not only achieve for your company, you will be happy for yourself.

In business, we have today very high competition, so to met the targets, one has to be very sharp, active, in good health, and should perform and win the game every day, it is a continuous process, and if you lose you lose everything in life, so win all the games.

Racing makes one a Super Hero.

100 Business Schools

HARVARD, Stanford, London Business School, MIT, INSEAD, Columbia Business School, Yale School of Management are some of the best B-schools in the world. In India we have Indian Institute of Management Bangalore, Ahmedabad, Calcutta, Kozhikode, Indore, SP Jain, XLRI-Jamshedpur, Faculty of Management Studies-Delhi, Management Development Institute, Gurgaon, and many best B-schools, all have best rankings.

All IIMs produce the best future super managers who are ready every year to create a lot of job opportunities for others. They help in boosting the industry and the economy of the nation, they start their journey from management trainees and climb till they become managing directors of respected business houses in the country, & some become best entrepreneurs. Learning at IIMs is great, because students come and join with great talents and abilities, when all talents and abilities meet at one place, we get many ideas, many ideas deals to many business plans, and many business plans makes many companies, and many companies makes super industries, that's the beauty of studying at IIMs in India. They all bring in future change and many brands, many companies, and help in overall development of the nation. As far as I have seen all IIM pass outs have brought in quality changes in the country. They have not only contributed to their companies but have also contributed their bit for the nation, that's the benefit of studying at IIMs. At the same time all other institutes in India are also doing well and are also producing super business heroes.

Having a management degree really helps for everyone - you get to learn all management subjects and their applications in business, you develop good soft skills, leadership qualities, you bring in overall change, you get fat compensation packages, helps one to start his own business, you can go global, you start working in teams, you develop managerial qualities, to learn how to make the best use of available resources, other career opportunities, growth, respect in society, personal satisfaction, your parents friends and relatives admire you, most important is all contribute directly to the growth of the nation, our India.

Isn't it interesting, so go take up your admission at best B-schools for MBA.

HAPPY MBA NATION MBA is FUN Da

www.ingramcontent.com/pod-product-compliance
Lightning Source LLC
Chambersburg PA
CBHW071415170526
45165CB00001B/285